Packers
Triviology

Christopher Walsh

TRIUMPH
B O O K S

For Matt and Sarah, because it all began in Wisconsin.

"There are three important things in life: family, religion, and the Green Bay Packers."

—Vince Lombardi

Library of Congress Cataloging-in-Publication Data

Walsh, Christopher J., 1968–
  Packers triviology / by Christopher Walsh.
      p. cm.
  ISBN 978-1-60078-620-4
  1. Green Bay Packers (Football team)—Miscellanea. I. Title.
  GV956.G7.W25 2011
  796.332'640977561—dc22
                                        2011017191

This book is available in quantity at special discounts for your group or organization. For further information, contact:

Triumph Books
542 South Dearborn Street
Suite 750
Chicago, Illinois 60605
(312) 939-3330
Fax (312) 663-3557
www.triumphbooks.com

Printed in U.S.A.
ISBN: 978-1-60078-620-4
Design by Patricia Frey
Photos courtesy of AP Images except where otherwise noted

Contents

One

The Basics

About the only thing that's typical about the meeting is that it's held every year, come rain or shine, just like a football game.

On Thursday, July 29, 2010, NFL commissioner Roger Goodell joined 8,300 others, mostly wearing green and yellow, at Lambeau Field for the annual stockholders meeting. In addition to hearing the team's financial presentation—as the Green Bay Packers are the only major professional team required to disclose its financial information to the public—he answered some presubmitted questions from fans, including Beth Lohr of De Pere, Wisconsin, asking if she could have a hug. (The answer was yes.)

Green Bay Packers, Inc. has been a publicly owned, nonprofit corporation since August 18, 1923, when the original articles of incorporation were filed with Wisconsin's secretary of state. As of this writing 4,750,937 shares were owned by 112,158 stockholders, none of whom receive any dividend on the initial investment, or will ever get anything if the shares appreciate in value.

Incidentally, the financial report delivered in 2010 by team president and CEO Mark Murphy indicated that the Packers had an operating profit of approximately $9.8 million in the fiscal year that ended March 31, down from $20.1 million the previous year. In part due to investment losses, the team reported net income of approximately $5.2 million, up from $4 million.

It's a far cry from 1919, when Curly Lambeau received $500 from his sponsoring employer, the Indian Packing Company, for uniforms and equipment just two weeks before the team's first game.

1. What did co-founder George Calhoun initially call the team?
2. What did he also call the team, albeit briefly, in 1919?
3. What sponsorship essentially made the Packers' nickname permanent?
4. What color were the jerseys?
5. What NFL team has had its nickname longer?
6. What did Green Bay wear for the first time in 1950?
7. Who dubbed Green Bay "Titletown"?
8. Where do the players stay during training camp?
9. Before staying home in Green Bay, in what three locations did the Packers hold training camp?
10. What first did the Packers do in 1940 for a road game?
11. How did some of the players react to that?
12. Who designed the "G" logo for the helmets?
13. How many times has the organization changed it?
14. What are the only two pro sports franchises to have longer home-field tenures than the Packers at Lambeau Field?
15. Who created the Lambeau Leap?
16. Against which team did he score?
17. Among all the now-defunct teams that the Packers played, which was the only one they didn't beat?
18. What was Green Bay's largest margin of victory?
19. What's the biggest loss?
20. How many times have the Packers won three straight titles?
21. How many times have all the other teams in league done it?
22. True or false? The Packers have season-ticket holders from all 50 states.
23. True or false? The wait list for season tickets exceeds the capacity of Lambeau Field.
24. How long is the estimated wait?

Answers

1. The Indian Packers
2. The Indians
3. Acme Packing Co. In 1921 the team jerseys had "Acme Packers" on the front.
4. Blue
5. None. The Chicago Bears are the second oldest, 1922.
6. Green
7. Jack Yuenger, the *Green Bay Press-Gazette* advertising manager, after the 1961 championship.
8. St. Norbert College in De Pere, Wisconsin
9. Rockwood Lodge (Bayshore area, north of Green Bay, 1946–1949); Grand Rapids, Minnesota (1950–1953); University of Wisconsin–Stevens Point (1954–1957).
10. Green Bay was the first NFL team to fly to a road game. Fearing an accident, the league forced the Packers to split into two groups and fly separate DC-3s.
11. They took out life-insurance policies.
12. Equipment manager "Dad" Braisher
13. Zero
14. The Boston Red Sox at Fenway Park dates back to 1912, and the Chicago Cubs have played at Wrigley Field since 1914.
15. LeRoy Butler
16. It was against the Los Angeles Raiders on December 26, 1993. Reggie White recovered a fumble (which was caused by Butler), and then lateraled the ball to Butler, who went in for the touchdown.
17. The Baltimore Colts. The Packers were 0–1–0 against them before the franchise folded after the 1950 season. It was replaced in 1953 by the current Colts, who relocated to Indianapolis in 1984.
18. 53 points, 56–3 against Atlanta on October 23, 1966, at Milwaukee.
19. 56 points, 56–0 at the Baltimore Colts on November 2, 1958.
20. Twice: 1929, 1930, 1931 and 1965, 1966, 1967.
21. Zero
22. True, along with Washington D.C., Canada, Japan, and Australia.
23. True (as of 2011)
24. 40 years

Two

Famous Firsts

It began with a casual conversation on a street corner and a few weeks later led to a meeting in the editorial room of the *Green Bay Press-Gazette*. Curly Lambeau and George Calhoun wanted to start a football team and were motivated to make it a reality.

Little did they know that their 1919 meeting would become the foundation for one of the most unique and successful franchises in professional sports. Lambeau's employer, the Indian Packing Company, agreed to put up the money for jerseys and equipment in exchange for the team being named after it. The company also let the team use its athletic field for practice.

While the Indian Packing Company didn't last long, the Green Bay Packers found a way to survive through the years. They began as an independent club, but joined the American Professional Football Association in 1921. A year later the association was renamed the National Football League.

Financial difficulties plagued the team early on, eventually leading a group of local businessmen known as "the Hungry Five" to back the franchise and form the Green Bay Football Corporation.

Publicly owned, it held stock sales to help keep the team afloat and raise money over the years, including for construction of the stadium that would become known as Lambeau Field.

1. What date is considered the franchise's birthday?
2. Which team was the first opponent? (non-league play)
3. What was Green Bay's record its first season, 1919?
4. Which team was credited with the NFL championship that year?
5. True or false? Green Bay won its first NFL game.
6. Where was that first league game played?
7. Who threw the first official pass in franchise history?
8. For whom was it intended?
9. Who had the first reception?
10. Who scored the first touchdown?
11. Who threw the first touchdown pass in Packers history?
12. Who caught it?
13. Who kicked the first field goal in Green Bay history?
14. Who kicked the first extra point?
15. Against which team was the first defeat?
16. Who won the first meeting between the Packers and the Chicago Bears?
17. When did the Packers beat the Bears for the first time?
18. Which team did the Packers face in their first playoff game, and what was the outcome?

Answers

1. August 11, 1919
2. The North End Athletic Club. The Packers won 53–0.
3. 10–1
4. No one, because the NFL didn't exist yet. Canton was credited with winning the closest thing, the Ohio League championship.
5. True, 7–6 over the Minneapolis Mariners on October 23, 1921.
6. Hagemeister Park, Green Bay
7. Curly Lambeau
8. Lyle "Cowboy" Wheeler. It was incomplete.
9. Buff Wagner for 18 yards
10. Fullback Art Schmaehl on a four-yard run.
11. Curly Lambeau
12. Bill DuMoe, 35 yards on a fake kick vs. the Hammond Pros, November 13, 1921, at Hagemeister Park.
13. Curly Lambeau
14. Curly Lambeau
15. 13–3 to the Rock Island Independents, October 30, 1921, at Hagemeister Park
16. Chicago (which was then known as the Staleys) won 20–0.
17. 1925, in their fourth meeting.
18. The 1936 NFL Championship against the Boston Redskins was Green Bay's first NFL playoff game. It won 21–6.

Three

Stadiums

When the Green Bay Packers first organized in 1919, their home games were played at Hagemeister Park, located on the northern end of Washington Park near Baird and Walnut Streets, adjacent to the East River.

Once owned by Hagemeister Brewery, it was basically just a big lot, the kind where kids might wile away the days, dreaming of potential greatness and athletic accomplishments galore.

There was only the field, a painted gridiron, and a roped off area for spectators to stand. There were no gates, no bleachers, not even a fence. Some would drive up and sit atop their parked cars, but most would walk along the sideline to follow the action.

With no budget other than its original sponsorship, a hat was passed around for donations, but the Packers were successful enough that they would soon go from being an independent club to joining a league.

A year later, a small grandstand was built on one side of the field, with a fee charged for those who wished to sit. In 1921, a portable canvas fence was erected so that admission could be charged. It didn't last, though. The park was dug up in 1923 to make way for East High School and the Packers found themselves in need of a new home.

1. After Hagemeister Park, where did the Packers play home games in 1923–1924?
2. What was the park's primary purpose?
3. The inadequacies for football led to creation of what facility?
4. Where was it located?
5. Where would the Packers dress for games?
6. Where would visiting teams frequently dress?
7. Whose father supervised several expansions at both Hagemeister Park and City Stadium?
8. Which team was the first opponent at City Stadium? (Bonus: List the result.)
9. In 1933, where did the Packers play a home game for the first time? (Bonus: Name the opponent and result.)
10. What's now at that site?
11. In 1934, what became the Packers' second home?
12. What was the stadium's informal name?
13. What was the last game there?
14. Where did the Packers play their "Milwaukee" games the following year?
15. What subsequently became the Packers' Milwaukee home until 1994?
16. When was the last game played at City Stadium?
17. After numerous renovations, what was the capacity?
18. Why was it considered the league's best playing surface?
19. When a new stadium was dedicated on September 29, 1957, who participated in the pregame ceremony?
20. What was its capacity?
21. Which opponent did the Packers defeat that day?
22. Since 1968, what's the address for Lambeau Field?

Answers

1. Bellevue Park
2. It was a minor-league baseball park.
3. City Stadium
4. Behind the new high school.
5. In the school
6. In their hotel rooms, which they preferred to the high school.
7. Curly Lambeau's father, Marcel, who was a construction foreman.
8. The Hammond Pros. Green Bay won 14–0.
9. Milwaukee, at Borchert Field, a minor-league baseball stadium where the Packers attracted 12,467 fans. They lost the New York Giants 10–7.
10. A children's playground
11. State Fair Park, on the Wisconsin Fairgrounds
12. The Dairy Bowl
13. Green Bay lost to the Los Angeles Rams 28–0 in 1951.
14. The Packers played three games at Marquette Stadium in 1952. They defeated the Washington Redskins 35–20, lost to the Los Angeles Rams 30–28, and beat the Philadelphia Eagles 12–10.
15. County Stadium
16. November 18, 1956, a 17–16 loss to the San Francisco 49ers.
17. 25,000
18. The close proximity to the East River
19. Vice-president Richard Nixon, Miss America, and actor James Arness
20. 32,150
21. The Chicago Bears, 21–17
22. 1265 Lombardi Avenue

Four

Nicknames

The Green Bay Packers are sort of an unusual franchise in that while the players have rarely had famous nicknames, there are all sorts of monikers associated with the team itself.

Because of the number of championships, Green Bay is commonly referred to as "Titletown."

It naturally gets so cold in northeast Wisconsin that the field is described as the "Frozen Tundra"—and since this is a trivia book, the term "tundra" is derived from the Kildin Sami word tundâr, which means "uplands" and "treeless mountain tract" (though Green Bay does have trees it is obviously lacking in mountains).

If someone scores a touchdown they may do the "Lambeau Leap" while "Cheesehead" fans wave their "Title Towels."

You get the idea.

As for the team nickname, when the franchise was founded Curly Lambeau solicited funds from his employer, the Indian Packing Company, to sponsor the team. Later, the ACME Packing Company did the same, and that's why there are some famous, old team pictures with "ACME Packers" across the front of the jerseys.

Quiz!

Try to come up with the popular nicknames for the following players/coaches.
(FYI, some are much tougher than others)

1. Clay Matthews III
2. B.J. Raji
3. Aaron Rodgers
4. Roy Marlon Baker

5. Larry McCarren
6. Jim Bowdoin
7. Reggie White
8. Brett Favre

Aaron Rodgers and Clay Matthews celebrate their Super Bowl XLV victory over the
Pittsburgh Steelers.

9. Larry Gantt
10. Bernard Darling
11. Earl Lambeau
12. Edmund Bratkowski
13. Ray Nitschke
14. John Cochran
15. Joseph Dunn
16. Lavern Dilweg
17. Francis Earp
18. Earl Girard
19. Paul Engebretsen
20. Charles Goldenberg
21. Joel David Hanner

22. Carl Jorgensen
23. Chester Johnston
24. Mike Michalske
25. Czeslaw Marcol
26. Buford Ray
27. Earl Svendsen
28. Fred Thurston
29. Howard Woodin
30. Paul Hornung
31. Vince Lombardi
32. Kabeer Gbaja-Biamila
33. Johnny McNally
34. Vince Workman

Answers

1. The Claymaker
2. The Freezer
3. Mr. Rodgers, although some have called him A-Rod.
4. Bullet, but also known as Snowy and Ironsides
5. The Rock
6. Goofy
7. The Minister of Defense
8. The Gunslinger (Although he had many other nicknames when finishing his career with the rival Minnesota Vikings, but we can't print them here.)
9. Superman
10. Boob
11. Curly
12. Zeke
13. Wildman
14. Red
15. Red
16. Lavvie
17. Jug
18. Jug
19. Tiny
20. Buckets
21. Hawg
22. Bud
23. Swede
24. Iron Mike
25. Chester
26. Baby
27. Bud
28. Fuzzy
29. Whitey
30. Golden Boy
31. The Pope
32. KGB
33. Blood
34. Pookie

Five

Jersey Numbers

What's in a number? Sometimes a lot. When *Sports Illustrated* put together its list of the best NFL players by jersey numbers five Green Bay Packers were named:

No. 4: Brett Favre
No. 15: Bart Starr
No. 31: Jim Taylor
No. 64: Jerry Kramer
No. 66: Ray Nitschke

How many of them have had their jersey numbers retired by the Packers? Two.

We'll start with the obvious questions. (FYI, the Packers have no listing of jersey numbers for players before 1925, when they first appeared in game programs. All questions are through 2009 unless specifically noted otherwise.)

Quiz!

1. How may Green Packers have had their number retired?
2. Name them.
3. What were their numbers?
4. List the order in which they were retired.
5. Who has worn the most numbers on the Packers?
6. Who's worn the second most?
7. Through 2009, what's been the most popular number worn by players?
8. Who wore it the longest?
9. Who is the only player in Green Bay history to wear No. 1?
10. Who were the only two players to wear No. 2?
11. Brett Favre was the fifth player to wear No. 4. Who were the first four?
12. Who has worn No. 6 longer than one season?
13. Which two Hall of Famers wore No. 14 before Don Hutson?
14. During his two stints as Brett Favre's backup, what number did Doug Pederson wear?
15. Why did fullback William Henderson wear No. 33?
16. Who was the first player to wear No. 42?
17. Who wore it the longest?
18. Who was the last player to wear No. 66?
19. Who was the last player to wear No. 69?
20. Who wore No. 71 the longest?
21. Who was the last player to wear No. 92 before Reggie White?
22. What was the last number given out by the Packers?
23. Heading into the 2011 season, who has worn No. 12 the longest in Packers history?
24. What number did future Packers head of college scouting John Dorsey wear as a player?
25. Name the three players for whom the Packers have no documentation which numbers they wore.

Answers

1. Five
2. Tony Canadeo, Don Huston, Ray Nitschke, Bart Starr, and Reggie White
3. Tony Canadeo, 3; Don Huston, 14; Ray Nitschke, 66; Bart Starr, 15; and Reggie White, 92.
4. Don Huston, 1951; Tony Canadeo, 1952; Bart Starr, 1973; Ray Nitschke, 1983; Reggie White, 2005.
5. Mike Michalske, with nine (19, 24, 28, 30, 31, 33, 36, 40, 63).
6. Arnie Herber, with eight (12, 16, 19, 26, 38, 41, 45, 68).
7. No. 23, 35 players have worn it.
8. Three players wore it for five years, guard Whitey Woodin (1927–1931), end Clyde Goodnight (1945–1949), and safety Tiger Green (1986–1990).
9. Curly Lambeau, 1925–1926
10. Charlie Mathys, 1925–1926 and Mason Crosby, 2007–2010
11. Verne Lewellen, 1925–1926; Herm Schneidman, 1935–1937; Chuck Fusina, 1986; Dale Dawson, 1988
12. No one
13. Curly Lambeau, 1927 and Johnny "Blood" McNally, 1933–1934
14. No. 18.
15. Religious reasons. According to the Bible, Jesus was crucified at age 33.
16. Curly Lambeau in 1928.
17. Darren Sharper, from 1997–2004.
18. Nose tackle Mike Lewis in 1980, before it was retired in honor of Ray Nitschke.
19. Guard Jeff Blackshear in 2002.
20. Santana Dotson
21. Nose tackle John Jurkovic
22. No. 96, which was first worn in 1987 by defensive end Tony Leiker.
23. Zeke Bratkowski, 1963–1968, 1971
24. No. 98
25. Guard Adolph Bieberstein (1926), back Eddie Kotal (1925), and back Jim Crowley (1925)

Six

Records

In many NFL media guides the section on individual records begins with a bit of a disclaimer that should always be taken into consideration when it comes to season and career statistics.

In 1960, the regular season lasted just 12 games, which probably would have been a little disappointing to Green Bay fans had they known what was coming. The Packers' 40th season in the National Football League resulted in an 8–4 record, which was good enough to win the Western Division, but they lost to Philadelphia 17–13 in the NFL Championship Game.

It would be the team's only championship loss under the direction of Vince Lombardi.

With the addition of the expansion Minnesota Vikings in 1961, the regular season was increased to 14 games, which the league maintained through 1977.

In 1978, with fans complaining about having to pay for several preseason games in addition to the regular season as part of their ticket packages, the league added two more games to the schedule in addition to a second wildcard for the playoffs so that more teams would still be in contention for the postseason during the final weeks of the season.

It should also be noted that coaches didn't start tracking Packers defensive statistics until 1975.

Just something to keep in mind when looking over the numbers.

1. Who had the longest tenure with the Packers as an active player?
2. Who played in the most games?
3. Who had the longest tenure among defensive players?
4. How many seasons did Don Hutson lead the league in scoring?
5. Who holds the team record for the most consecutive seasons leading the Packers in scoring?
6. Who holds the NFL record for points in a single quarter?
7. Who made the longest run from scrimmage in team history?
8. Which quarterback holds the team record for passes intercepted in a single season?
9. Through the 2010 season, who's made the most tackles in Packers history?
10. Who holds the team record for tackles in a single season?
11. Where does Bart Starr's 104.80 career postseason passer rating rank in NFL history?
12. Who holds the franchise record for most seasons leading the team in total tackles?
13. Who holds the Packers record for most unassisted tackles in a single season?
14. True or false? Brett Favre holds the team record for consecutive pass attempts without an interception.
15. True or false? Brett Favre holds the NFL record for the most passes intercepted in a single season.

16. Who holds the NFL record for most games with 20 completions and no interceptions?
17. True or false? When Green Bay lost to Arizona in a 2009 wildcard game, Jermichael Finley's 159 receiving yards set an NFL record for receiving yards by a tight end in a postseason game.
18. What's the longest reception by Packers tight end?
19. Who holds the team single-season record for tackles by a defensive lineman?

Name the individual team record holders in the following categories. (Bonus: List the numbers too.)

20. Career rushing yards
21. Career passing yards
22. Career passing touchdowns
23. Career receiving yards
24. Career receiving touchdowns
25. Career interceptions
26. Career field goals
27. Career touchdowns
28. Career sacks
29. Season rushing yards
30. Season passing yards
31. Season passing touchdowns
32. Season receptions
33. Season receiving yards
34. Season interceptions
35. Season touchdowns
36. Season points
37. Season sacks

Answers

1. Bart Starr (1956–1971) and Brett Favre (1992–2007) both played 16 seasons with the Packers.
2. Brett Favre played 255 games—all consecutive—compared to Bart Starr's 196.
3. Ray Nitschke (1958–1972)
4. Five, which is an NFL record.
5. Ryan Longwell, with nine
6. Don Hutson, who scored four touchdowns and kicked five extra points for 29 points in the second quarter against Detroit on October 7, 1945.
7. Ahman Green, 98 yards vs. Denver on December 28, 2003
8. Lynn Dickey, with 29 in 1983
9. John Anderson, 1,020, 1978–1989
10. Nick Barnett, with 194 in 2005
11. It is the highest career postseason passer rating in history.
12. Nick Barnett, five times
13. Rich Wingo, with 151 in 1979
14. False, and it's not close. Bart Starr had 294 passes without an interception, while Brett Favre's best streak was 163.
15. False. George Blanda holds the record with 42 in 1962.
16. Brett Favre, with 65. He also has the record for most games with 30 pass attempts and no interceptions (61), and is tied with Drew Bledsoe for most games with 40 pass attempts and no interceptions (15).
17. False, it was second to San Diego's Kellen Winslow (166 yards, January 2, 1982, vs. Miami)
18. Paul Coffman had a 78-yard touchdown reception in 1979.
19. Aaron Kampman, with 113 in 2006
20. Career rushing yards: Ahman Green, 8,322, 2000–2006
21. Career passing yards: Brett Favre, 61,655, 1992–2007
22. Career passing touchdowns: Brett Favre, 442, 1992–2007
23. Career receiving yards: James Lofton, 9,656, 1978–1986
24. Career receiving touchdowns: Don Hutson, 99, 1935–1945
25. Career interceptions: Bobby Dillon, 52, 1952–1959
26. Career field goals: Ryan Longwell, 277 (1997–2005)
27. Career touchdowns: Don Hutson, 105 (1935–1945)
28. Career sacks: Kabeer Gbaja-Biamila, 74.5, 2000–2008
29. Season rushing yards: Ahman Green 1,883 yards, 2003
30. Season passing yards: Lynn Dickey, 4,458, 1983
31. Season passing touchdowns: Brett Favre, 39, 1996
32. Season receptions: Sterling Sharpe, 112, 1993
33. Season receiving yards: Robert Brooks, 1,197, 1995
34. Season interceptions: Irv Comp, 10, 1943
35. Season touchdowns: Ahman Green, 20, 2003
36. Season points: Paul Hornung, 176, 1960
37. Season sacks: Tim Harris, 19.5, 1989

Seven

Quotes

When thinking of the Green Bay Packers, the last thing that probably comes to mind is the glitz and glamour of Hollywood. In fact, Titletown may be the closest thing to the opposite of Tinseltown.

However, the two have crossed paths before.

For example, the 2008 movie *Leatherheads*, starring George Clooney and Renee Zellweger, was inspired by Hall of Famer Johnny "Blood" McNally. Brett Favre made a hilarious cameo in the comedy *There's Something About Mary*. The Packers were the subject of a 1937 MGM/UA movie, *Pigskin Champions*. Former Packer and Lambeau Field announcer Gary Knafelc was an actor who used the screen name Gary Kincaid. Actor Matthew McConaughey's father, Jim, was drafted by the Packers (27th round, 1953) as was Alan Autry, who played Captain Bubba Skinner in the TV series *In the Heat of the Night*.

However, the marquee Hollywood appearance by a Green Bay Packer has to be Ray Nitschke, who starred as Guard Bogdanski in the 1974 Burt Reynolds movie *The Longest Yard*. His character is memorably carried from the field after being drilled in a, shall we say, sensitive area by two bullet passes from Paul "Wrecking" Crewe.

Quiz!

Name the person who made the following statements, (and if you don't know the answer it's probably Vince Lombardi.)

1. "I'm pretty boring really."
2. "There is no substitute for work; it is the price of success."
3. "Everything we talk about is about beating the Packers, the Bears, and the Vikings. Obviously there are other teams in the league, but if you can dominate and be on top of your division you are always in the playoff hunt. It's time for us to win that thing."
4. "Coach, did you ever play in this league?"
5. "Just call me the judge. All I do is sit on the bench."
6. "Fatigue makes cowards of us all."
7. "We hitched our wagon to a Starr."
8. "There are certain guys you want to hit, and some you don't. I try to take everyone's head off, to tell the truth. I'm not going to play differently regardless. I'm out there to play 100 percent every play, whoever it is. If it was my own brother, I wouldn't change my play."
9. "Let's get one thing straight right now: I'm in complete command here."
10. "The Packers have lots of owners nobody knows instead of one owner who doesn't know squat."
11. "If I ever play on this field again, I'll jump off the Empire State Building."
12. "Ed Neal weighed 275 pounds, stripped. His arms were as big as my leg and as hard as a table."
13. "What people said couldn't happen here, happened here. I'm proud of that."
14. "Two or three plays in a game spell victory or defeat. You never know when that play is coming up."
15. "I also played in the 1967 Super Bowl against the Green Bay Packers."
16. "The things he can do with his arm and his feet. It's hard to find someone better right now."

17. "We have been accused of playing mean, vicious, hungry football. It has been said we only play to win. How else is there to play?"
18. "When you played for Vince Lombardi, anything other than death was a minor injury."
19. "Gentlemen, I've never been associated with a losing team. I do not intend to start now"
20. "I had pro offers from the Detroit Lions and Green Bay Packers, who were pretty hard up for linemen in those days. If I had gone into professional football [my] name might have been a household word today."
21. "Football is a game of inches and inches make a champion."
22. "It was the character of the Packers, man. We played for 60 minutes. We let it all hang out. There was no tomorrow for us. We got the adrenaline flowing, and we just let it go, man."
23. "About 10 vodkas."
24. "There wasn't a better teacher or mentor out there than Reggie White, on or off the field."
25. "Our greatest glory is not in never falling, but in rising every time we fall. If the defense is scattered all over the field, it means that they are either confused, tired, or without desire."
26. "Teamwork is what the Green Bay Packers were all about. They didn't do it for individual glory. They did it because they loved one another."
27. "We're just a fart in the wind. This ought to take care of all that silly dynasty talk."
28. "The guy's got nothing to prove. He's the best quarterback I've ever seen. He can certainly go out in style. We'll wait and see, but it's pretty emotional. It's weird to think of the Green Bay Packers without him."
29. "Physical pressure on an opponent is necessary. Mental pressure will make him crack."
30. "I'm not a madman."
31. "Many things have been said about Coach, and he is not understood by those who quote him. The players understand. This is one beautiful man."

32. "You know the old saying, when it rains it pours. When it comes, it comes in bunches. It seems that way in my case."
33. "I want to hug him more than strangle him, but it's close,"
34. "Maybe winning isn't everything, but it sure comes way ahead of whatever is second."
35. "You never lose a game if your opponent doesn't score."
36. "That was probably the most brutal football game that I have ever been in. I know that it was. The weather was terrible, and the field was frozen, and the wind in Yankee Stadium was just terrible. It really was the coldest that I ever played in. The weather affected me more than the Ice Bowl game that was played in Green Bay."
37. "A winning football team must avoid mistakes with a passion, treat mistakes with a vengeance."
38. "I would still rather score a touchdown than make love to the prettiest girl in the United States."
39. "I was brought here to win."
40. "Desire is cold fury burning within a man."
41. "I've enjoyed every minute of my 15 years, well almost every minute. There is nothing I could have done with my life that I would have enjoyed more. There is only one thing I regret, looking back: I regret that it is not 1958 again, so I'd have it do over again."
42. "Classic example of Dr. Jekyll and Mr. Hyde."
43. "The harder a man works, the harder it is to surrender."
44. "Lombardi was a cruel, kind, tough, gentle, miserable, wonderful man, who I often hate, often love, and always respect."
45. "Good fellows are a dime a dozen. Aggressive leaders are priceless."
46. "Sometimes you get caught up in what's going on around you. The reality is that you are just a regular person. At some point, the career will be over, the bright lights turn off. That can come back to haunt you if you're not just a regular guy."
47. "Pursuit is an all-out effort on defense."

48. "Reggie White was the ultimate player at his position for two decades. To have a player of that caliber cast with your players speaks volumes for your team and the direction you want to take with your organization. You're talking about a man selected to 13-straight Pro Bowls."
49. "There doesn't look to be any limit to what he can do."
50. "Defeat must be admitted before it is reality."
51. "We are not familiar with losing, and that is one thing we stress in this locker room: don't get familiar with losing, because we never lose games here."
52. "I just love to play football."
53. "We're always trying to find ways to lower interceptions and stuff. My nature, I'm aggressive. I'll take shots, I'll take chances; therefore, you have mistakes."
54. "Anything is ours providing we're willing to pay the price."
55. "When it's third and long, you can take the milk drinkers and I'll take the whiskey drinkers every time."
56. "When I wanted to hire Ted—I've told people this story—he was the one I wanted and I called Ron Wolf before I made the final call to Ted. I said, 'If I want someone to come in for me and do what you did for me in 1991, do you have someone you recommend?' He said, 'Ted Thompson.'"
57. "Mental attitude is 75 percent of winning."
58. "Every man must leave the field with the feeling that every spectator is convinced they have seen the best player in the country."
59. "Lambeau was always special, and so was Milwaukee."
60. "I told all of the coaches here that we had two of the most physical safeties in the country playing behind me. I knew if I didn't make the tackle they were probably going to hit me on their way to make the tackle. So I had to get there first, before them."
61. "It's crazy. I don't want to say you feel violated, but everybody's touching you all over the place. I've got both legs up, with some people grabbing one leg while some other people were tugging on the other leg. I've never had so many hands on me. But I've got nothing to hide."
62. "When I got there, this was the worst team in professional football."

63. "Want it, desire it, earn it, take it."

64. "You're never guaranteed about next year. People ask what you think of next season, you have to seize the opportunities when they're in front of you."

65. "I'll play anywhere for $15,000."

66. "There's a great deal of love for one another on this club. Perhaps we're living in Camelot."

67. "Winning is a habit."

68. "It is a dream come true. It's what I dreamt about as a little kid watching Joe Montana and Steve Young, and we just won the Super Bowl."

69. "I'm the only man with a Dallas Cowboys Super Bowl ring who doesn't wear it. I'm a Green Bay Packer."

70. "Confidence is contagious. So is a lack of confidence."

71. "Packer fans are nuts, man."

Answers

1. Brett Favre
2. Vince Lombardi
3. Steve Mariucci
4. 1987 first-round draft pick Brent Fullwood to Forrest Gregg.
5. Ray Nitschke, on being a backup player his first year under Vince Lombardi.
6. Vince Lombardi
7. Jim Taylor on Bart Starr
8. A.J. Hawk
9. Vince Lombardi
10. Jim McMahon
11. Don Hutson after the 1944 season, only to play again the following year.
12. Bulldog Turner, who had his nose broken five times by Ed Neal.
13. Ron Wolf
14. Vince Lombardi
15. Jim Otto
16. Chad Clifton on Aaron Rodgers
17. Vince Lombardi
18. Bart Starr
19. Vince Lombardi
20. President Gerald R. Ford
21. Vince Lombardi

Fans congratulate Vince Lombardi after the Packers upset the Chicago Bears in Lombardi's first game as Green Bay's head coach on September 27, 1959. *(Getty Images)*

22. Ray Nitschke
23. Fuzzy Thurston, on how he prepared for the Ice Bowl.
24. Brett Favre
25. Vince Lombardi
26. Vince Lombardi
27. Ron Wolf
28. Ryan Longwell on Brett Favre.
29. Vince Lombardi
30. Ray Nitschke
31. Jerry Kramer on Vince Lombardi.
32. Brett Favre
33. Mike Holmgren

34. Vince Lombardi
35. Vince Lombardi
36. Ray Nitschke on the 1962 NFL Championship Game
37. Vince Lombardi
38. Paul Hornung
39. Ron Wolf
40. Vince Lombardi
41. Ray Nitschke
42. Bart Starr on Ray Nitschke
43. Vince Lombardi
44. Jerry Kramer
45. Vince Lombardi
46. Brett Favre
47. Vince Lombardi
48. Ron Wolf
49. Pete Carroll on Clay Matthews III
50. Vince Lombardi
51. Donald Driver
52. Ray Nitschke
53. Brett Favre
54. Vince Lombardi
55. Max McGee
56. Bob Harlan
57. Vince Lombardi
58. Vince Lombardi
59. Ray Nitschke
60. A.J. Hawk
61. Aaron Rodgers
62. Ron Wolf
63. Vince Lombardi
64. Brett Favre
65. Herb Adderley after being asked if he'd rather play Super Bowl II in Los Angeles or Miami.
66. Jerry Kramer
67. Vince Lombardi
68. Aaron Rodgers
69. Herb Adderley
70. Vince Lombardi
71. Ray Nitschke

Eight

Nearly 100 Years' Worth of Questions

Anniversaries can be a tricky thing. Don't believe it? Try forgetting one and see what happens.

For the team's 50th anniversary, a list of greatest Packers was compiled.

50th Anniversary Team:

Offense: Don Hutson, end; Boyd Dowler, end; Cal Hubbard, tackle; Fred "Fuzzy" Thurston, guard; Jim Ringo, center; Jerry Kramer, guard; Forrest Gregg, tackle; Bart Starr, quarterback; Paul Hornung, running back; Clarke Hinkle, running back; Jim Taylor, running back; Larry Craig, end; Lavvie Dilweg, end; Willie Davis, end.

Defense: Robert "Cal" Hubbard, tackle; Henry Jordan, tackle; Dave Hanner, tackle; Ray Nitschke, linebacker; Dave Robinson, linebacker; Bill Forester, linebacker; Herb Adderley, defensive back; Jesse Whittenton, defensive back; Bobby Dillon, defensive back; Willie Wood, defensive back.

Speaking of anniversaries, here are some questions celebrating the almost 100 years of Packers history.

1919: At the end of the season the players split the profits. How much did each get?

1922: Why was Green Bay briefly kicked out of the American Professional Football Association?

1927: In addition to being elected district attorney of Brown County, which includes Green Bay, who led the Packers in rushing?

1932: How were the Chicago Bears able to claim the NFL title despite having seven wins compared to the Packers' 10?

1935: A year before the NFL's first draft, what key player did Green Bay sign? (Bonus: What school did he attend?)

1938: What key rookie addition helped lead Green Bay to the West Division title?

1939: Which addition helped extend the career of Don Hutson, even though he sustained a knee injury?

1945: Who came out of retirement to score nine touchdowns and kick 31 extra points and two field goals?

1948: Why did Curly Lambeau fine the entire team half of one week's salary?

1955: Who was the only player in the league to have more rushing yards than Howie Ferguson's 859?

1957: Who did Packers fans think might be a bust after bouncing around in the backfield and playing three different positions?

1962: What was the only game Green Bay lost all season? (Hint: It was played on November 22.)

1965: When Green Bay and Baltimore finished atop the Western Division with identical 10–3–1 records, how was the tie broken?

1967: With Jim Taylor and Paul Hornung gone and the backfield sustaining numerous injuries, who led the Packers in rushing?

1970: Which happened first: Vince Lombardi's death or Phil Bengtson's resignation as coach of the Packers?

1971: What happened to Dan Devine during his first game coaching the Packers?

1976: In Green Bay's five wins, how many times did it have to come from behind in the second half?

1977: After quarterback Lynn Dickey sustained a broken leg, who stepped in and led Green Bay to wins in two of its last three games?

1979: After an impressive preseason, who sustained a knee injury a couple minutes into the opener and was lost for the season?

1982: In Bart Starr's only playoff appearance as a coach, which team(s) did the Packers face?

1986: After numerous veterans were let go in an effort to get younger, what was the only non-division opponent that Green Bay defeated?

1987: Which future Packers scout was selected by the Houston Oilers third overall in the 1987 NFL draft behind Cornelius Bennett and Vinny Testaverde?

1989: Who led the team in interceptions despite being 36?

1992: Who did Mike Holmgren join when he became just the third Green Bay coach to have a winning record in his first season?

1993: How many game-winning catches did wide receiver Sterling Sharpe have?

1994: Which three Packers were named to the NFL's 65th Anniversary Team?

1995: Who was "reluctantly" cut during the off-season?

1997: What accomplishment was Brett Favre the first player to pull off in NFL history?

2000: Who was the only Green Bay player named to the Pro Bowl?

2002: Which opposing team was the first to win a playoff game at Lambeau Field?

2003: What was so memorable about Green Bay's 41–7 victory at Oakland on *Monday Night Football*?

2004: True or false? Brett Favre had his most passing yards with the Packers with 4,088.

2007: What prominent anniversary did the Packers celebrate?

2008: Which team did Aaron Rodgers beat in his first start quarterbacking the Packers?

2010: Which former prominent Packer played with the Omaha Nighthawks of the United Football League?

Brett Favre hands off to Ahman Green during a 2002 game against the Redskins.
(Getty Images)

Answers
1919: $16.75
1922: Because the Packers used two active Notre Dame players in a non-league game against the Chicago Supremes. Green Bay was reinstated after apologizing and paying a $250 franchise fee.
1927: Verne Lewellen
1932: Ties didn't count in the standings. Chicago was 7–1–6 (.875), while Green Bay was 10–3–1 (.769).
1935: Don Hutson from Alabama.

1938: Cecil Isbell

1939: Larry Craig

1945: Don Hutson

1948: The fine was for "indifferent play" during a 17–7 loss to the Chicago Cardinals (who went 11–1 that season). When players didn't get their money back after winning the subsequent game, 16–0 over the Los Angeles Rams, the Packers went 1–7 the rest of the season, and Curly Lambeau finally reimbursed the players in January.

1955: Baltimore Colts rookie fullback Alan Ameche, with 961.

1957: Paul Hornung, the Heisman Trophy winner from Notre Dame.

1962: The Detroit Lions, 26–14.

1965: The division title was decided in a playoff, with the Packers winning in overtime 13–10.

1967: Jim Grabowski, with 466 yards on 120 carries and two touchdowns.

1970: Lombardi died on September 3, while Bentson resigned December 21.

1971: Several players smashed into Devine on the sideline and broke his leg during a 42–40 loss to the New York Giants.

1976: Four

1977: Rookie David Whitehurst

1979: Fullback Eddie Lee Ivery

1982: Green Bay beat the St. Louis Cardinals 41–16 but then lost at the Dallas Cowboys 37–26.

1986: Cleveland, 17–14. Green Bay also defeated Tampa Bay twice and Detroit once.

1987: Alonzo Highsmith

1989: Dave Brown

1992: Curly Lambeau and Vince Lombardi

1993: Three

1994: Don Hutson, Ray Nitschke, and Reggie White.

1995: Sterling Sharpe, after sustaining a neck injury the previous season.

1997: Favre was named league MVP for the third straight year.

2000: Darren Sharper

2002: The Atlanta Falcons, led by quarterback Michael Vick.

2003: Brett Favre's father, Irvin, died of a heart attack the day before the game. Favre elected to play and passed for four touchdowns in the first half, and finished with 399 yards.

2004: False. He passed for 4,413 yards in 1995.

2007: The season marked the 50th anniversary of Lambeau Field, tying the NFL record for most seasons at one venue. The Chicago Bears played 50 seasons at Wrigley Field (1921–1970).

2008: The Minnesota Vikings, who went 10–6 and won the division, while the Packers finished 6–10.

2010: Ahman Green

Nine

Draft/Trades

It pretty much goes without saying that many Green Bay Packers fans consider tackle Tony Mandarich to not only be the worst draft pick in franchise history, but perhaps the worst draft pick ever.

They have good reason. In 1989, he was tabbed by *Sports Illustrated* as "the best offensive line prospect ever," a notion shared by numerous NFL officials. Consequently, the Packers used the second-overall selection on him instead of Barry Sanders, Derrick Thomas, Deion Sanders...you get the idea.

Mandarich, of course, never panned out, and three years later was cut. He eventually returned to the NFL, played three years with the Indianapolis Colts, but admitted in 2008 to taking steroids and having reported to the Packers addicted to a drug called Staydol.

But was he really the worst pick in Packers history?

Is he worse than Randy Duncan, who chose the British Columbia Lions of the Canadian Football League over the Packers? Or Rich Campbell, who only appeared in seven games over four years? What about Bruce Clark? Larry Elkins? How about Florida State defensive end Jamal Reynolds? After winning the Lombardi Award with the Seminoles he recorded just one sack over two seasons.

Green Bay tried to trade him to the Indianapolis Colts, but instead was forced to cut him after he failed his physical.

Just something to think about.

1. Of all the Green Bay players in the Pro Football Hall of Fame, how many were drafted in the first round?
2. Who did the Packers select with their first-ever draft pick in 1936?
3. Who was the only player selected by the Packers in the 1944 draft to play for the team in his first eligible year?
4. Who was the first player to be drafted by the Packers in the first round who *didn't* play for them in his first eligible year?
5. True or false? The second player was in the following year.
6. Who was drafted twice by the Packers in 1948 and 1949?
7. What 1950 first-round pick—fifth overall—snubbed the Packers to play for the Ottawa Rough Riders for a season?
8. Which college teammate of his did Green Bay select the following year, fourth overall?
9. In 1956, when Green Bay drafted Forrest Gregg and Bart Starr, who did it pick in the first round?
10. Who was the only player to make the team after being selected in the 30th round?
11. Who holds the record as the highest draft pick to make the Packers?
12. In 1977, defensive end Ezra Johnson was selected in the first round out of what school?
13. Who did the Packers take in the first round of the 1984 USFL Supplemental Draft?
14. Who did Green Bay take in the second round of the 1998 Supplemental Draft?

15. Which two players selected first-overall by other teams ended up playing for the Packers at some point?

16. Which two players selected first-overall in the AFL Draft played for the Packers?

17. From which school has Green Bay made the most first-round selections?

18. Through 2009, what three positions had the Packers selected the most in the first round?

19. What did the Packers give up to get Ray Nitschke from the Giants?

20. What did Vince Lombardi give up to get Henry Jordan from Cleveland?

21. True or false? A year later he pried defensive end Willie Davis from the Browns for a fifth-round pick.

22. In 1966, what did Vince Lombardi give to Detroit in exchange for end Ron Kramer?

23. Who did Dan Devine trade away to get linebacker Ted Hendricks?

24. A year later, what did the Raiders send in a trade to the Packers for Ted Hendricks?

25. Who did that eventually turn into?

26. What did the Packers give up to acquire quarterback John Hadl from the Los Angeles Rams?

27. When Green Bay traded John Hadl away, who did it acquire?

28. In 1981, who did Green Bay acquire for wide receiver Aundra Thompson, a future first-round selection and two second-round picks?

29. In 1987, what did the Packers get in exchange for James Lofton?

30. Who did Green Bay acquire in exchange for its 1992 first-round selection, 17th overall?

31. When Ron Wolf traded a fourth- and eighth-round pick to San Francisco in 1993, what three players did they turn into?

32. How did the Packers get Donald Driver?

33. How did the Packers get Ahman Green?

Answers

1. Three (Paul Hornung, Herb Adderley, and James Lofton)
2. San Francisco guard Russ Letlow
3. Michigan guard Merv Pregulman
4. Marquette back Johnny Strzkalski, the sixth-overall selection in 1946
5. True, UCLA back Ernie Case, who was also the sixth-overall selection.
6. Nevada back Stan Heath, who was selected in the 25th round in 1948, and the first round in 1949, fifth overall.
7. Kentucky tackle Bob Gain, who then played from 1952–1964 with the Cleveland Browns.
8. Babe Parilli
9. Miami halfback Jack Losch
10. Southern California guard Al Barry, who was pick No. 355.
11. Colorado linebacker Mark Cooney made the team despite being selected with the 402nd pick, in the 16th round of the 1974 draft.
12. Morris Brown
13. McNeese State running back Buford Jordan with the 12th-overall selection (New Orleans Breakers).
14. Navy tackle Mike Wahle
15. Bobby Garrett and Russell Maryland
16. Jack Concannon and Jim Grabowski
17. Minnesota, with seven
18. Tackles (12), linebackers (nine), and quarterbacks (eight)
19. Defensive end John Martinkovic
20. A 1960 fourth-round draft choice
21. False, Lombardi gave up end A.D. Williams.
22. A first-round draft choice (fullback Jim Grabowski)
23. He acquired Ted Hendricks and a 1975 second-round draft choice (later sent to Los Angeles Rams in John Hadl trade) from the Baltimore Colts for linebacker Tom MacLeod and a 1975 eighth-round draft choice.
24. The Raiders sent two first-round draft choices to the Packers for the rights to Hendricks and then signed him as a limited free agent.
25. Green Bay used the two picks to select tackle Mark Koncar in 1976 and defensive end Ezra Johnson in 1977.
26. First-, second-, and third-round choices in 1975, and first- and second-round choices in 1976
27. Quarterback Lynn Dickey and defensive back Ken Ellis from the Houston Oilers, a 1976 fourth-round draft choice (through Philadelphia), and a 1977 third-round choice.
28. San Diego wide receiver John Jefferson
29. A 1987 third-round choice (wide receiver Frankie Neal) and a 1988 fourth-round selection (nose tackle Rollin Putzier) from Los Angeles Raiders.
30. Brett Favre, from the Atlanta Falcons
31. He acquired a fourth-round (running back Edgar Bennett), fifth-round (wide receiver Orlando McKay), and sixth-round (tight end Mark Chmura) selection.
32. Green Bay drafted him in the seventh round of the of the 1999 draft with the pick acquired from Chicago for running back Glyn Milburn.
33. Ron Wolf acquired him and a fifth-round selection from Seattle for cornerback Fred Vinson and a sixth-round pick.

Ten

Titletown

Although the Green Packers are renowned for their postseason play, the road to Super Bowl XLV included a stop that could only be described as historic.

For the first time the league's oldest rivalry was on display in the NFC Championship Game when the Packers visited the Chicago Bears. Game No. 182 in the series was arguably the biggest yet— but it wasn't their first postseason meeting.

In 1941, both teams were 10–1 atop the Western Division, having beaten each other once. Instead of a tiebreaker, they settled it in a rare playoff game at Wrigley Field on December 14, one week after the attack on Pearl Harbor.

After Chicago fumbled the opening kickoff and the Packers took an early lead on Clarke Hinkle's one-yard run, the Bears scored 30-straight points by halftime en route to a 33–14 victory. The Bears went on dominate the New York Giants 31–9, though the game's attendance of 13,341 was the smallest for any NFL title game.

In 2011, though, the Packers fared much better. Quarterback Aaron Rodgers passed for 266 yards and ran in a touchdown, but his biggest contribution may have been the touchdown-saving tackle of linebacker Brian Urlacher after a third-and-goal interception. The defense held, and the Packers went on to a 21–14 victory.

It was just the fourth time that both teams participated in the playoffs during the same season, and marked just the fifth time since the 1970 AFL-NFL merger that the Packers faced a team from their division in the postseason.

Nevertheless, the Packers finished their playoff run with their 13th title and the best postseason winning percentage in NFL history (.644).

Sterling Sharpe en route to the end zone once again.

1929 (12–0–1, first place)

1. True or false? The Packers finished the previous season below .500.
2. Which three key players did Green Bay sign during the off-season?
3. Which team did Green Bay shut out in its season opener?
4. What team was the first to score against the Packers?
5. Which was the first opponent to score a touchdown?
6. How many points did Green Bay give up all season?
7. Which opponent(s) scored the most?
8. Which opponent(s) managed a scoreless tie?
9. Which team finished second in the standings at 13–1–1?
10. Which two key players missed that game due to injuries, and who left with an injury during the final minute of play?
11. How many points did the Chicago Bears score in three losses to the Packers? (Bonus: Give the combined points for Green Bay.)
12. Who was Green Bay's leading rusher?
13. How many more rushing yards did he have over teammate Verne Lewellen?
14. How many more rushing yards did Verne Lewellen have over teammate Bo Molena?
15. Who led the lead the team in passing with 501 yards?
16. Who had the most touchdown passes?
17. Who led the team with 20 receptions for 297 yards?
18. What local college did he attend?
19. True or false? Green Bay played its first five games at home and its final eight on the road.
20. How was the team welcomed home?

Answers

1. False, Curly Lambeau led his team to a 6–4–3 finish.
2. Future Hall of Famers Johnny "Blood" McNally, Cal Hubbard, and Mike Michalske
3. The Dayton Triangles, 9–0
4. The Chicago Cardinals, on a safety.
5. The Chicago Cardinals in their second of three meetings that season, during the Packers' sixth game. Green Bay gave up just three touchdowns all season.
6. 22
7. The Chicago Cardinals, Minneapolis Red Jackets, and New York Giants all scored six points.
8. The Frankford Yellow Jackets on Thanksgiving Day.
9. The New York Giants, which Green Bay defeated 20–6 on November 24.
10. Red Dunn and Eddie Kotal missed the game, and Jim Bowdoin was sidelined during the final minute.
11. Zero, compared to 62 combined points by the Packers.
12. Johnny "Blood" McNally, with 406 yards
13. One, although he led the Packers in rushing touchdowns with six.
14. Four
15. Verne Lewellen
16. Hurdis McCrary had five, while Verne Lewellen had four.
17. Eddie Kotal
18. Lawrence
19. True
20. Roughly 20,000 celebrated all night in freezing temperatures when the Packers arrived home by train on December 9.

1930 (10–3–1, first place)

1. True or false? Green Bay was the first team to win back-to-back NFL championships.
2. Which opponent snapped Green Bay's 23-game unbeaten streak that dated back to 1928, with a 13–6 victory on November 16.
3. Which team unintentionally helped out the Packers on that same day by upsetting the 8–1 New York Giants?
4. Which opponent beat Green Bay by the exact same score the following week?
5. What Army standout made his professional debut that game?
6. Which team did Green Bay defeat 37–7 on November 30 to essentially clinch the league title?
7. Which team did they tie in the season finale to win a second-consecutive NFL championship?
8. Who led the team in rushing with 458 yards?
9. Who was right behind him with 405 and had seven rushing touchdowns?
10. Who took over the team lead in passing?
11. Which number was greater: his touchdown passes or interceptions?
12. What statistic did Johnny "Blood" McNally lead the Packers in?
13. Who led the team with six interceptions?
14. In which statistical category did opponents have a significant advantage?
15. True or false? Green Bay played its first seven games at home and its final seven on the road.
16. In the *Green Bay Press-Gazette*'s annual All-NFL team, which was chosen by polling writers, team officials and coaches, how many Packers were on the first-team?
17. Name them.
18. True or false? Green Bay was the first team in NFL history to win the league title with three losses or more.

Answers

1. False, the Chicago Bears did it first.
2. The Chicago Cardinals
3. The Chicago Bears
4. The New York Giants
5. Chris Cagle
6. The Staten Island Stapletons
7. The Portland Spartans
8. Bo Molenda
9. Verne Lewellen
10. Red Dunn
11. Red Dunn had nine touchdown passes and seven interceptions.
12. Receiving, with 22 catches for 410 yards and four touchdowns.
13. Lavie Dilweg
14. Punt returns. The Packers were outgained 526 yards to 283.
15. True
16. Two
17. Lavie Dilweg and Mike Michalske
18. True

1931 (12–2, first place)

1. What two veterans did Curly Lambeau add from the New York Giants?
2. Who did the Packers acquire at midseason to strengthen the line even more?
3. How many points did the Packers score?
4. How many teams scored within 100 points of that?
5. Whose injury slowed the Packers' offense?
6. Which team gave up fewer points than Green Bay's 87?
7. True or false? For the fourth-straight year the Packers' defense intercepted at least 30 passes.
8. For the second year in a row, what player burned Green Bay in its first loss?
9. Which team did he do the same to the following week, seriously hurting their championship hopes?
10. Why did the Packers (12–2) refuse to play the Portsmouth Spartans (11–3) in the season finale on December 13, which would have decided the NFL title?
11. Consequently, against which opponent did Green Bay close the season and what was the result?
12. In which two categories did Johnny "Blood" McNally lead the league?
13. In what defensive category did he lead the Packers?
14. True or false? Green Bay had 1,000-plus rushing yards more than its opponents.
15. True or false? Opponents outpassed Green Bay, 1,469 to 1,041.
16. Which team did Green Bay defeat 26–0 in its season opener?
17. What opponent managed to score 20 points in a losing effort?
18. True or false? Green Bay was the first team in NFL history to win three straight titles.
19. Which team ended Green Bay's dynasty a year later with a 19–0 home victory on December 4, 1932?
20. Why? (Bonus: Name the team it became.)

Answers

1. Linemen Dick Stahlman and Rudy Comstock
2. Center Nate Barranger from the Frankford Yellow Jackets
3. 291
4. None
5. Verne Lewellen
6. The Portsmouth Spartans yielded just 77.
7. True
8. Ernie Nevers of the Chicago Cardinals, who won 21–13.
9. The Portsmouth Spartans
10. Green Bay argued that the game was not on the official league schedule, and an early date was only tentatively scheduled between the teams, so either side had the right to cancel it. NFL president Joe Carr agreed with the Packers, thus essentially awarding them the championship.
11. Green Bay lost at the Chicago Bears 7–6.
12. Receiving touchdowns (11) and points scored (84)
13. Interceptions, with six.
14. True, 2,337 compared to 1,333.
15. False, reverse the numbers.
16. The Cleveland Indians
17. The Providence Steam Rollers, which scored only 78 points all season.
18. True
19. The Portsmouth Spartans
20. Because even though Green Bay would have more wins at the end of the 1932 season, with 10, ties didn't count toward the standings. When the Chicago Bears beat Portsmouth in a playoff game and won the league title with a 7–1–6 record, the NFL approved an annual championship game. In 1934, the owner of a Detroit radio station purchased the Spartans, moved them and changed the nickname to Lions.

1936 (Packers 21, Redskins 6)

1. What major innovation did the NFL implement that season?
2. In which category did the Packers lead the league during the regular season: most points scored or fewest points allowed?
3. What was the outcome when the Packers and Redskins met during the regular season?
4. What was the only team to beat Green Bay that season?
5. True or false? Every team in the Western Division had a better record than the Redskins.
6. Who led the league in passing?
7. How many touchdown passes did he have?
8. True or false? He had more interceptions.
9. True or false? He also led the Packers in rushing yards.
10. Which two linemen were named All-Pro?
11. What position did Don Hutson play defensively?
12. Who did the Boston Redskins defeat to advance to the championship game?
13. Where was the championship game played?
14. Why?
15. What "first" did that represent in league history?
16. What did that end up being the precursor to?
17. Who scored the game-winning touchdown?
18. Who scored the final touchdown?
19. True or false? The 1936 season was the first since the formation of the NFL in which there were no franchise transactions.

Answers

1. The first draft was held.
2. Green Bay led the league in points scored with 248. The 118 points allowed were only fourth best.
3. Green Bay won at home 31–2, then won the rematch in Boston 7–3.
4. The Chicago Bears, on September 20, 30–3. Green Bay won the rematch in Chicago 21–10.
5. False. Green Bay, the Chicago Bears, and Detroit all did, but the Chicago Cardinals finished 3–8–1.
6. Arnie Herber, who completed 77 of 173 yards for 1,239 yards.
7. 11, which also led the league.
8. True, with 13
9. False. Herber had 36 yards rushing, while Clarke Hinkle led the Packers with 476 rushing yards.
10. Tackle Ernie Smith and guard Lon Evans
11. Defensive end. He would later move to safety.
12. The New York Giants, 14–0
13. The Polo Grounds in New York
14. Boston Redskins owner George Marshall had raised ticket prices on the day of a game without warning, drawing the ire of fans. So, due to poor attendance he moved the title game from Fenway Park to New York.
15. It was essentially the first NFL title game held on a neutral field.
16. The Redskins moved to Washington D.C. before the subsequent season.
17. Milt Gantenbein, on an eight-yard touchdown pass from Arnie Herber
18. Bob Monnett, on a two-yard run
19. True. It was also the first year that all teams played the same number of games.

1939 (Packers 27, Giants 0)

1. What important position change did Coach Curly Lambeau make?
2. How did he respond?
3. With the move, who was inserted?
4. Who led the Packers in passing?
5. Who led the team in rushing?
6. Which two teams beat Green Bay during the regular season?
7. True or false? They were the two closest games the Packers played.
8. Which team did the New York Giants beat in their regular-season finale to advance to the championship game?
9. How was the game decided?
10. Which team did Green Bay beat in the season finale to hold off the hard-charging Chicago Bears?
11. On average, how many points per game did the Giants give up during the regular season?
12. On average, how many points per game did the Packers score during the regular season?
13. Where was the title game played?
14. True or false? The title game set a home attendance record for the Packers.
15. Which two Packers caught touchdown passes?
16. Who ran in the final touchdown?
17. Who retired prior to the 1939 season only to return in 1940, and consequently never won an NFL Championship?
18. Who won the Pro Bowl game in Los Angeles between the Packers and the NFL All-Stars?

Answers

1. He moved Don Hutson on defense from end to safety.
2. Hutson led the league with 34 receptions for 846 yards, but perhaps more importantly it helped extend his career.
3. Rookie Larry Craig
4. Arnie Herber, with 1,107 yards, compared to Cecil Isbell's 749.
5. Cecil Isbell
6. The Cleveland Browns and Chicago Bears
7. False. Green Bay lost both games by three points. It defeated the Cleveland Browns 7–6 on November 26.
8. The Washington Redskins, 9–7.
9. Washington's Bo Russell missed a field-goal attempt with 45 seconds remaining.
10. Detroit, 12–7
11. 7.7, which led the league.
12. 20.3, which led the league.
13. Wisconsin State Fair Park in West Allis, near Milwaukee
14. True, with 32,279 fans. The gross receipts of $83,510.35 set a record.
15. Milt Gantenbein (seven yards) and Joe Laws (31 yards)
16. Ed Jankowski
17. Tackle Champ Seibold
18. Green Bay won 16–7.

1944 (Packers 14, Giants 7)

1. How long was Green Bay's winning streak to start the season?
2. Against which team did the streak start?
3. Who led the Packers in passing?
4. How many players had more than 100 rushing yards?
5. Who had the most?
6. How many rushing touchdowns did he have?
7. How many times had Don Hutson led the league in touchdowns, setting an NFL record?

8. In which category did the Packers lead its division: passing yards or interceptions?
9. How many points did the Packers score in their two losses?
10. Which notable former Packer played for the Giants?
11. How many years had he been retired?
12. How did one reporter refer to him after he reported to training camp?
13. Which team did the Giants defeat 31–0 in the regular-season finale to clinch the Eastern Division?
14. True or false? The Giants' 75 points allowed were half as many as any other team in the league.
15. Who scored two touchdowns in the championship game—one on a pass, the other a one-yard run?

1961 (Packers 37, Giants 0)

1. To which team did Green Bay lose in its season opener?
2. How many weeks were the Packers not in at least a tie for first place in the Western Division?
3. Why did Paul Hornung miss the November 19 game against the Los Angeles Rams?
4. What happened a few days later when the Packers visited the Detroit Lions?
5. For the first time in league history, where was an NFL title game played?
6. Despite the location, what revenue milestone was reached for the first time?
7. What major equipment decision was made by both teams before the game?
8. Which key Green Bay Packer played despite injuring a kidney two weeks earlier?
9. Which two defensive players had key second-quarter interceptions that set up touchdowns?
10. Who scored them?
11. Of those players, which two were also on leave from Fort Lewis?
12. What unusual incident occurred during Green Bay's first possession of the second half?
13. Who scored 19 points, an NFL record for a championship game?
14. What was the Packers' turnover differential that year?
15. Which number was greater: Giants rushing yards or Packers penalty yards?
16. True or false? It was the first time the league championship was a shutout.
17. True or false? It was the last time the league championship was a shutout.

Answers
1. The Detroit Lions, 17–13
2. Just two, and after improving to 5–1 the Packers were alone atop the division for the rest of the season.
3. Due to construction of the Berlin Wall, the U.S. Department of Defense activated thousands of reservists, including Paul Hornung.
4. Paul Hornung was flown from Fort Riley to Detroit for the game, where he kicked a field goal and two extra points in a 17–9 victory.
5. Green Bay, Wisconsin. (When the Packers hosted the 1939 title game it was played near Milwaukee.)
6. It was the first NFL championship to generate $1 million.
7. With the temperature dipping to −15 degrees two days before the game, a tarp was kept on the field until game day. The Packers wore cleats and many of the Giants wore sneakers, believing they would grip better.
8. Jim Taylor
9. Ray Nitschke and Hank Gremminger
10. Boyd Dowler, on a 13-yard pass, and Ron Kramer, on a 14-yard run.
11. Ray Nitschke and Boyd Dowler
12. Officials accidentally gave Green Bay a fifth down. However, the Packers still ended up punting.
13. Paul Hornung
14. +20
15. The Giants ran for 31 yards, while the Packers had 16 penalty yards.
16. False. The Packers beat the Giants 27–0 to win the 1939 title.
17. False.

1962 (Packers 7, Giants 0)

1. Green Bay went undefeated at home for the first time since what year?
2. Which opponent was the only one to beat the Packers?
3. How many yards did the Packers gain during a 49–0 victory against Philadelphia?
4. Which Packer led the league in their respective individual category: Bart Starr in passing yards, Jim Taylor in rushing yards, or Willie Wood in interceptions?
5. True or false? The Packers led the league in fewest points allowed, with 148.
6. Where was the championship game played?
7. Despite this, for what was the game remembered?
8. Which team did it favor and why?
9. Out of the 65,000-plus tickets sold, how many were no-shows?
10. How did broadcaster Art Rust Jr. later describe the conditions?
11. What set up Green Bay's first touchdown, a seven-yard run by Jim Taylor?
12. What was the game's longest pass completion?
13. Of Green Bay's five fumbles, how many did the Giants recover?
14. Who intercepted a Y.A. Tittle pass near the end zone?
15. How did the Giants score their only touchdown?
16. Who kicked three field goals for the Packers?
17. Who said, "I don't remember ever being hit so hard. I bled all game. They really came to play."
18. Who called it the hardest game he ever played in?
19. Which New York Giant said, "We're still the better team."
20. Who was named MVP of the championship game?

Answers

1. 1944
2. The Detroit Lions, 26–14.
3. 628, compared to 54 allowed.
4. All three did. Starr passed for 2,438 yards, Taylor had 1,474 rushing yards, and Wood made nine interceptions.
5. True
6. Yankee Stadium
7. The frigid conditions, magnified by 35-mph wind gusts. Television crews used bonfires to thaw out their equipment and one photographer sustained frostbite.
8. The Packers, which were more run-oriented.
9. 299
10. "Barbaric"
11. Ray Nitschke recovered a Phil King fumble on the Giants' 28, which was followed by a halfback-option pass from Paul Hornung to flanker Boyd Dowler.
12. A 25-yard gain from Y.A. Tittle to Joe Walton.
13. None
14. Dan Currie, on a ball tipped by Ray Nitschke.
15. Erich Barnes blocked a Max McGee punt which Jim Collier fell on in the end zone.
16. Guard Jerry Kramer
17. Jim Taylor
18. Paul Hornung
19. Frank Gifford
20. Ray Nitschke

1965 (Packers 23, Browns 12)

1. Against which team in the season finale did Green Bay blow a chance to clinch the division by tying it 24–24?
2. After finishing tied atop the Western Division, which team did Green Bay beat in overtime in a winner-takes-all playoff game?
3. Who fumbled on the first play of that game?
4. Perhaps more importantly, who was hurt on the play and missed most of the game?
5. Who kicked the game-tying and game-winning field goals?
6. True or false? Many observers claimed the winning field goal actually went wide.
7. Where was the championship game played?
8. What television-first occurred with the game?
9. Who had more rushing yards in the game: Jim Brown or Jim Taylor?
10. How did Green Bay have so much success stopping the Cleveland running back?
11. What adjustment did Vince Lombardi call for to make things more difficult for Browns receiver Paul Warfield?
12. How did the Packers get the Browns on their heels?
13. How did Green Bay fans respond to Cleveland's first touchdown, a 17-yard reception by Gary Collins?
14. How long was Green Bay's drive in the third quarter that ended with Paul Hornung's 13-yard touchdown run?
15. Who knocked the ball out of Jim Brown's hands in the end zone to end Cleveland's last touchdown threat?
16. Who made a touchdown-saving tackle on kick returner Leroy Kelly in the fourth-quarter?

17. Who made the last-minute interception to seal the victory?
18. How many penalties were called in the game?
19. Who made two field goals for the Browns, but was unsuccessful on his first extra-point attempt (due to a botched snap) and had a field goal deflected by Forrest Gregg?
20. The game was the last for which prominent player?

Answers

1. The San Francisco 49ers
2. The Baltimore Colts, 13–10.
3. Bill Anderson, with Don Shinnick returning it 25 yards for a touchdown.
4. Bart Starr
5. Don Chandler
6. True
7. Lambeau Field
8. It was the first NFL championship broadcast in color.
9. Actually, it was Paul Hornung, who had 105 rushing yards on 18 carries. Jim Taylor notched 96 on 27 carries, and Jim Brown was limited to 50 yards on 12 carries.
10. Ray Nitschke shadowed him, and in the poor conditions the Packers clogged up the middle to force him to take extra steps while looking for openings.
11. He had Bob Jeter, who was faster and could better keep up, cover Warfield instead of Doug Hart.
12. Green Bay came out throwing, with Carroll Dale's 47-yard reception giving the Packers a quick 7–0 lead.
13. They threw snowballs at Collins.
14. 90 yards on 11 plays.
15. Ray Nitschke
16. Don Chandler
17. Herb Adderley
18. Five, three on the Packers.
19. Lou Groza
20. Jim Brown

Super Bowl I (Packers 35, Chiefs 10)

1. What was the game initially called?
2. Who later came up with the term "Super Bowl"?
3. Where was the game played?
4. True or false? It's the only Super Bowl that was not a sellout.
5. How much did tickets cost?
6. Which team was favored?
7. Which team did Kansas City defeat in the AFC Championship Game?
8. Which three key defensive players were acquired in a trade with Cleveland?
9. Who boasted the week before the game that he would use his "hammer" (i.e., his forearm) to destroy the Green Bay receivers?
10. Which league's game ball was used?
11. Which network broadcasted the game?
12. What was the cost of a 30-second commercial?
13. Why did the Chiefs receive a second kickoff at the start of the season half, which cost it nearly 30 yards of field position?
14. How did that possession end?
15. Who scored on the next play?
16. True or false? After that point the Chiefs never crossed midfield.
17. Who scored the first touchdown in Super Bowl history?
18. Which injured player had he replaced on the 80-yard drive?
19. Who was named game MVP?
20. How much did the Packers get for winning the Super Bowl?

Answers

1. The AFL-NFL World Championship Game
2. Kansas City Chiefs owner Lamar Hunt
3. Los Angeles Memorial Coliseum
4. True. Attendance was announced at 61,946.
5. $12, which prompted negative editorials from the local newspapers about the high price.
6. The Packers by 14 points.
7. It beat the Buffalo Bills 31–7.
8. Willie Davis, Henry Jordan, and Bill Quinlan
9. Chiefs cornerback Fred "the Hammer" Williamson
10. Both. When the Chiefs were on offense they used the AFL ball by Spaulding, while the Packers used the NFL ball by Wilson.
11. Both NBC and CBS showed the game.
12. $42,000 on either network.
13. NBC had not returned in time from a commercial break for the second-half kickoff, which the Chiefs had returned to near midfield.
14. After moving the ball to its own 49-yard line, quarterback Len Dawson was intercepted by Willie Wood, who returned it 50 yards in a key momentum swing.
15. Elijah Pitts on a five-yard run
16. False, but only for one play.
17. Max McGee, on a 37-yard touchdown reception
18. Boyd Dowler
19. Bart Starr. He completed 16 of 23 passes for 250 yards, two touchdowns, and one interception.
20. $15,000 for each player

Bart Starr hands off in Super Bowl II against the Raiders. *(Getty Images)*

Super Bowl II (Packers 33, Raiders 14)

1. Where was the game played?
2. Which team was favored?
3. What did the halftime show feature?
4. After having just three interceptions during the previous regular season, how many did Bart Starr have in 1967?
5. How many points did Green Bay give up through its first 11 games, when it clinched its division?
6. Who coached the Oakland Raiders?
7. Who did they crush in the AFC championship?
8. What was their defense nicknamed?
9. Who scored the first touchdown on a 62-yard play-action pass?
10. Who kicked three field goals in the first half?
11. True or false? It was the last game of his career.
12. Who said in the locker room at halftime, "Let's play the last 30 minutes for the old man."
13. Whose final reception of his career, for 35 yards, set up a two-yard touchdown run by Donny Anderson?
14. Who knocked Bart Starr out of the game with a sack that jammed Starr's thumb?
15. What happened on Zeke Bratkowski's lone pass attempt?
16. Who had the first interception return for a touchdown in Super Bowl history?
17. Who missed part of the second half while looking for a lost contact on the sideline? (Hint: He was the game's leading rusher.)
18. Which number was greater: Green Bay turnovers or penalties?
19. True or false? Bart Starr was named Super Bowl MVP for the second-straight year.
20. Since then, who is the only player to be named Super Bowl MVP two straight years?

1. The Orange Bowl in Miami
2. The Packers, by 13½ points
3. The Grambling State marching band
4. 17, compared to nine touchdown passes, even after missing four games due to injuries.
5. 131 (8.4 average), only to yield 78 the final three games (26.0).
6. John Rauch
7. The Houston Oilers, 40–7
8. The 11 Angry Men
9. Boyd Dowler
10. Don Chandler
11. True
12. Jerry Kramer
13. Max McGee, who subsequently retired
14. Ben Davidson
15. He was sacked
16. Herb Adderley, on a 60-yard return.
17. Ben Wilson
18. The Packers had no turnovers and just one penalty.
19. True
20. Terry Bradshaw, Super Bowls XIII and XIV

Super Bowl XXXI (Packers 35, Patriots 21)

1. Where was the game played?
2. Which team was favored?
3. What story about Bill Parcells broke mere days before the game?
4. Which team did the Patriots beat in the AFC Championship Game?
5. Which team did the Packers beat in the NFC Championship Game?
6. True or false? Brett Favre was the league's MVP.
7. In which category did the Packers lead the league: points scored or fewest points allowed?
8. Between Dorsey Levens, William Henderson, and Edgar Bennett, who led the team in rushing during the regular season?
9. Which of those three led the team in rushing yards during the Super Bowl?
10. Who was honored with helmet decals worn by both teams?

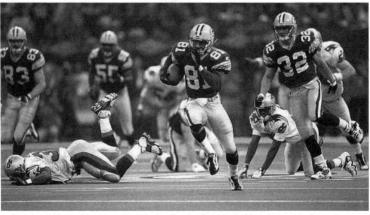

Desmond Howard turns on the jets, leaving the Patriots behind during his Super Bowl-record 99-yard kickoff return for a touchdown. *(Getty Images)*

11. True or false? The Packers were the first team in Super Bowl history to win in a dome while wearing its dark-colored jerseys.
12. How many times did the Packers intercept a Drew Bledsoe pass?
13. Who set a Super Bowl record with three sacks?
14. Who scored on Green Bay's second offensive play?
15. Who was called for pass interference to help set up New England's first touchdown, but later came back to make an interception?
16. Who set a Super Bowl record with an 81-yard touchdown reception?
17. True or false? Desmond Howard's 99-yard kick return for a touchdown is the longest play in Super Bowl history.
18. Who was named Super Bowl MVP?
19. His selection represented what Super Bowl first?
20. What two single-game Super Bowl records did he set?
21. True or false? Brett Favre was the first quarterback to score three touchdowns and win a Super Bowl and not be named the game's MVP.
22. How many consecutive Super Bowls had the NFC won?
23. Who played the halftime show?
24. Who died while practicing for the show?

Answers

1. Louisiana Superdome in New Orleans, Louisiana
2. The Packers were favored by 14 points
3. That Parcells would leave the Patriots after the Super Bowl to become the head coach of the New York Jets.
4. The second-year Jacksonville Jaguars, 30–6.
5. The second-year Carolina Panthers, 30–13.
6. True, for the second straight season.
7. Both. The Packers scored 456 points and allowed 210, becoming the first team since the 1972 Miami Dolphins to lead the league in both categories.
8. Edgar Bennett, with 899 rushing yards
9. Dorsey Levens, with 61 rushing yards
10. Former NFL commissioner Pete Rozelle, who had died on December 6, 1996.
11. True, the previous seven games in domes were all won by the team wearing white.
12. Four
13. Reggie White
14. Andre Rison, on a 54-yard pass
15. Craig Newsome
16. Antonio Freeman
17. False, it is the second longest. The longest is James Harrison's 100-yard interception return for a touchdown in Super Bowl XLIII.
18. Desmond Howard. He finished with 154 kick-return yards and 90 punt-return yards.
19. He was the first special-teams player to be named Super Bowl MVP.
20. Total return yards and combined net yards gained, with 244.
21. True
22. 13
23. James Brown, ZZ Top, and the Blues Brothers
24. Laura "Dinky" Patterson, a member of a professional bungee-jumping team

Super Bowl XLV: Green Bay 31, Pittsburgh 25

1. Where was the game played?
2. Which team was favored?
3. Who botched the Star-Spangled Banner?
4. What was noticeably absent from the sidelines?
5. Coming in, how many of its previous 10 playoff games had Pittsburgh won?
6. Who was the only NFL quarterback to have a better career postseason winning percentage than Ben Roethlisberger's .833?
7. Who were the first five quarterbacks in NFL history to start three Super Bowls in their first seven seasons, with Ben Roethlisberger becoming the sixth?
8. Before the Packers, how many times had a No. 6 seed in the NFC playoffs advanced to the Super Bowl?
9. Which is the only AFC team to accomplish that?
10. Who was Pittsburgh's only Pro Bowl selection on offense?
11. In which category did Pittsburgh's defense lead the league: sacks, fewest points, or rushing yards allowed?
12. Who was named the NFL Defensive Player of the Year?
13. After President Barack Obama said he would attend the Super Bowl if the Chicago Bears won the NFC Championship Game, who said in a postgame speech: "The President don't want to come watch us at the Super Bowl. Guess what? We're going to see him" and then broke the meeting with a team cheer of "White House!"?
14. What did the Packers do as part of their team meeting the night before the game?
15. Who scored the first touchdown of the game?
16. How many teams have come back to win a Super Bowl after having an interception returned for a touchdown?

17. Who did it for Green Bay?
18. True or false? Green Bay became the first team in NFL history to score a touchdown on an interception return in each of three consecutive postseason games.
19. Who caught a touchdown pass right before halftime to close Pittsburgh's deficit to 21–10?
20. Who was the game's leading rusher?
21. What was the only Super Bowl record set in the game? (Note: Tied records don't count.)
22. How many turnovers did the Packers have?
23. How many turnovers did the Steelers have?
24. How many times has the team that made more turnovers won the Super Bowl?
25. How many first downs by penalty did the teams combine to record?
26. How many different Packers scored in the postseason to set an NFL playoff record?
27. Who did Aaron Rogers join to become just the second NFL quarterback with 1,000 yards passing and nine touchdown passes in one postseason?
28. Which team, between Green Bay and Pittsburgh, which are ranked first and second, has the league's best all-time postseason winning percentage?
29. What off-field issue turned into a public relations nightmare?
30. Who was named Super Bowl MVP?
31. True or false? Green Bay never trailed by more than seven points at any point of the season.
32. What was the last team to complete a season with that distinction?
33. How many people in the Unites States watched the game on television?

Answers

1. Cowboys Stadium in Arlington, Texas
2. Packers by 2½
3. Christina Aguilera
4. Cheerleaders. The Steelers haven't had cheerleaders since 1970, and Green Bay hasn't since 1988.
5. Nine
6. Bart Starr, who was 9–1 (.900).
7. Troy Aikman, Tom Brady, John Elway, Bob Griese, and Jim Kelly.
8. None, the Packers were the first.
9. The Steelers were the No. 6 seed when they won Super Bowl XL.
10. Rookie center Maurkice Pouncey, who didn't play in the Super Bowl due to injury.
11. All three. The Steelers led the NFL in sacks (48), fewest points (14.5), and rushing yards (62.8) allowed per game.
12. Safety Troy Polamalu
13. Charles Woodson
14. The players were fitted for their ring sizes.
15. Jordy Nelson
16. None, they're 0–11.
17. Nick Collins
18. True
19. Hines Ward
20. Rashard Mendenhall, with 64 rushing yards and a touchdown.
21. Fewest combined rushing attempts with 36. The Packers had 13 and the Steelers 23.
22. None
23. Three
24. Just three
25. Zero
26. Eleven different Packers scored touchdowns in the playoffs. The previous mark of 10 was held by the 1940 Chicago Bears, 1985 New England Patriots, and 1992 Dallas Cowboys.
27. Kurt Warner, with 1,147 passing yards and 11 touchdowns in 2008. Rogers had a four-game total of 1,094 passing yards and nine touchdowns.
28. Green Bay tops the league at 29–16 (.644), with Pittsburgh at 33–20 (.623).
29. Roughly 400 people didn't have a seat.
30. Aaron Rogers completed 24 of 39 passes for 304 yards and three touchdowns.
31. True
32. The 1962 Detroit Lions
33. According to the Nielsen Company the game had a total audience of 162.9 million viewers, making it the most-watched show in U.S. television history.

Eleven

Hall of Fame

In 1961, the decision was made to build the Pro Football Hall of Fame in Canton, Ohio, the 1920 birthplace of the American Professional Football Association. The league was later renamed the National Football League.

Canton was also where Jim Thorpe, perhaps the first big-name athlete to play the game, started his professional career with the Canton Bulldogs in 1915.

Being enshrined is considered the highest honor than can be bestowed in the sport, as evidenced by that inaugural class in 1963: Sammy Baugh, Bert Bell, Joe Carr, Earl "Dutch" Clark, Harold "Red" Grange, George Halas, Mel Hein, Wilbur "Pete" Henry, Robert "Cal" Hubbard, Don Hutson, Earl "Curly" Lambeau, Tim Mara, George Preston Marshall, John "Blood" McNally, Bronko Nagurski, Ernie Nevers, and Thorpe.

Since then, the building was expanded in 1971, 1978, and 1995, and renovated in 2003 and 2008. Today numerous people associated with the Green Bay Packers are forever honored there.

Quiz!

1. Put in order the Packers contingency in the Pro Football Hall of Fame by induction, first to most recent.
2. List the jersey numbers for each Hall of Fame player. (Note: For those who wore numerous numbers, the one they wore most.)
3. There are five other Hall of Fame Packers who were primarily linked to other teams. Name them. (Bonus: Name the years they played for the Packers.)
4. Name their jersey numbers with the Packers.
5. How many NFL teams have more people enshrined in the Pro Football Hall of Fame?

Answers

1. Earl "Curly" Lambeau, 1963; Don Hutson, 1963; Robert "Cal" Hubbard, 1963; John "Blood" McNally, 1963; Mike Michalske, 1964; Clarke Hinkle, 1964; Arnie Herber, 1964; Vince Lombardi, 1971; Tony Canadeo, 1974; Jim Taylor, 1976; Forrest Gregg, 1977; Bart Starr, 1977; Ray Nitschke, 1978; Herb Adderley, 1980; Willie Davis, 1981; Jim Ringo, 1981; Paul Hornung, 1986; Willie Wood, 1989; Henry Jordan, 1995; James Lofton, 2003; Reggie White, 2006

2. Herb Adderley, 26; Tony Canadeo, 3; Willie Davis, 87; Forrest Gregg, 75; Arnie Herber, 38; Clarke Hinkle, 30; Paul Hornung, 5; Robert "Cal" Hubbard, 40; Don Hutson, 14; Henry Jordan, 74; Earl "Curly" Lambeau, 1; James Lofton, 80; John "Blood" McNally, 24; Mike Michalske, 36; Ray Nitschke, 66; Jim Ringo, 51; Bart Starr, 15; Jim Taylor, 31; Reggie White, 92; Willie Wood, 24

3. Len Ford (1958), Ted Hendricks (1974), Walt Kiesling (1935–1936), Jan Stenerud (1980–1983), Emlen Tunnell (1959–1961)

4. Len Ford, 83; Ted Hendricks, 56; Walt Kiesling, 49; Jan Stenerud, 10; Emlen Tunnell, 45

5. Only one: the Chicago Bears

Herb Adderley

1. Where was Herb Adderley born?
2. Where did he attend high school?
3. Where did he play college football?
4. True or false? Adderley is the College Football Hall of Fame.
5. What position did he play in college?
6. In what statistic did he lead his college team in both 1959 and 1960?
7. Why did he switch positions?
8. Who said, "I was too stubborn to switch him to defense until I had to. Now when I think of what Adderley means to our defense, it scares me to think of how I almost mishandled him."
9. How many interceptions did Adderley have with the Packers?
10. How many interceptions did he return for touchdowns?
11. Who eventually tied that team record?
12. Whose pass did he intercept and return for a touchdown in a Super Bowl?
13. Which team did Adderley finish his career with?
14. Who was he traded to in 1973?
15. True or false? Adderley returned 120 kickoffs during his career.
16. What was he the only player in NFL history to do? (Hint: Think Super Bowls)
17. On how many championship teams did he play?
18. Who were the only other players to do that?
19. How many career interceptions did he have?
20. How many for touchdowns?

Answers
1. Philadelphia, Pennsylvania
2. Northeast High School in Philadelphia
3. Michigan State
4. False
5. Running back
6. Receptions. He also led the Spartans in rushing yards his junior year.
7. Adderley began his career as a running back, but switched to cornerback to replace an injured teammate. Also, the Packers already had Paul Hornung and Jim Taylor.
8. Vince Lombardi
9. 39, over nine seasons.
10. Seven
11. Darren Sharper
12. Daryle Lamonica
13. The Dallas Cowboys (1970–1972)
14. The Los Angeles Rams, but instead of reporting he retired.
15. True, for 3,080 yards and two touchdowns.
16. Adderley was the only player to appear in four of the first six Super Bowls.
17. Six
18. Green Bay teammates Fuzzy Thurston and Forrest Gregg
19. 48
20. Seven

Tony Canadeo

1. What's Tony Canadeo's full name?
2. Where was he born?
3. Where did he play college football?
4. What nickname did he have there?
5. Why?
6. True or false? Canadeo is the only person associated with Gonzaga in the College Football Hall of Fame.
7. Who is the only other person with ties to Gonzaga in the Pro Football Hall of Fame?

8. What two positions did he play for the Packers?
9. At which was he named All-NFL first?
10. For years, which teammate did he back up?
11. Why did Canadeo miss the 1945 season?
12. What was he the first Green Bay Packer to accomplish?
13. How many players had pulled that off in NFL history?
14. What was Green Bay's record that season?
15. True or false? Canadeo also made nine interceptions on defense.
16. Which number was greater: career rushing yards or career passing yards?
17. True or false? He finished his career with more than 10,000 multipurpose yards.
18. Where did Canadeo die on November 29, 2003?

Willie Davis

1. Where was Willie Davis born?
2. Where did be play college football?
3. True or false? Davis is enshrined in the College Football Hall of Fame.
4. Which team selected Davis in the 15ᵗʰ round of the 1956 draft?
5. What did he do for two years before joining that team?
6. What position did he mostly play?
7. Who moved him to the defensive line?
8. How did he end up with the Packers?
9. In his 10 years with Green Bay, how many consecutive games did Davis play?
10. How many consecutive games did he play during his career?
11. Although it wasn't an official statistic at the time, it's estimated that Davis had more than how many sacks?
12. How many sacks did Davis believe he made one season?
13. How many fumbles did he recover?
14. True or false? That's a team record.
15. True or false? Davis had no interceptions during his career.
16. What honor did Davis receive in 1986?
17. What honor did Davis receive in 1987?
18. Where did he earn his MBA degree in 1968?
19. True or false? Davis has served on the board of directors of numerous prominent businesses.
20. How many of Vince Lombardi's title-winning teams was Davis a part of?

Answers

1. Lisbon, Louisiana, on July 24, 1934.
2. Grambling State
3. False
4. Cleveland Browns
5. He played Army football.
6. Offensive tackle
7. Vince Lombardi
8. Davis was acquired in a trade.
9. 138
10. 162
11. 100
12. 25
13. 21
14. True
15. False, he made two.
16. The Walter Camp Man of the Year Award
17. NFL Alumni's Career Achievement Award
18. The University of Chicago Graduate School of Business
19. True
20. All five

Quiz!

Forrest Gregg

1. Where was Forrest Gregg born on October 18, 1933?
2. Where did he play college football?
3. True or false? Gregg is in the College Football Hall of Fame.
4. True or false? Gregg was considered small for his position.
5. What record did Gregg set in 1971?
6. To what position did he switch due to injury problems?
7. What major compliment did Vince Lombardi give to describe Gregg?
8. Which team did Gregg play for during his final season of 1971?
9. What was Gregg's last game as a player?
10. Which team did he first serve as an assistant coach?

Forrest Gregg roars from the sideline during a December game in 1960.
(Getty Images)

11. In addition to the Packers, which two NFL teams did he serve as head coach?

12. Which coach preceded him, and who succeeded him as the Packers head coach?

13. Who did Gregg coach in 1978?

14. Which Canadian team did he coach?

15. Which former Green Bay Packer succeeded him?

16. What other CFL team did he coach?

17. What was Gregg's best season coaching the Packers?

18. What was Gregg's best record coaching in the NFL?

19. Where did Gregg serve as head coach at the collegiate level?

20. Under what unusual conditions was he hired?

21. After the 1989 season, to what position was he named?

Answers

1. Birthright, Texas
2. Southern Methodist
3. False
4. True, he was 6'4", 249 pounds.
5. Gregg played in 188 consecutive games from 1956–1971.
6. Guard
7. "Best player I ever coached."
8. The Dallas Cowboys
9. Super Bowl VI
10. The San Diego Chargers
11. The Cleveland Browns (1975–1977) and Cincinnati Bengals (1980–1983)
12. Bart Starr and Lindy Infante, respectively
13. No one
14. The Toronto Argonauts (1979)
15. Willie Wood
16. The Shreveport Pirates (1994–1995)
17. 8–8 (which he did twice, 1984 and 1985)
18. In 1981, his Bengals went 12–4 and defeated San Diego in the AFC Championship Game 27–7. They lost Super Bowl XVI 26–21 to San Francisco.
19. His alma mater, Southern Methodist.
20. Gregg was hired to revive the Mustang football program after it received the "death penalty" from the NCAA.
21. Athletic director

Arnie Herber

1. Where was Arnold Charles Herber born?
2. Where did he attend high school?
3. While there, what unusual way of throwing a football did he start doing?
4. As a youth, what did he do to attend Green Bay Packers games?
5. Where did he initially play college football?
6. Where did he transfer?
7. In what round was he selected in the NFL Draft?
8. Instead, what did he do after college?
9. How did he end up joining the Packers?
10. How much was his contract worth?
11. What position did he initially play?
12. True or false? The Packers won the NFL championship during Herber's first year.
13. In which category did Herber lead the league in both 1932 and 1933, when the NFL started keeping statistics?
14. What was he the first player in the NFL to do?
15. The addition of what key player significantly aided that?
16. Who did Herner start sharing playing time with during his final years in Green Bay?
17. After 11 seasons with the Packers what major decision did Herner make in 1940?
18. What caused him to change his mind in 1944?
19. Which team did he finish his career with?
20. Which team did they lose to in the 1944 title game?
21. How many NFL championships did he win with the Packers?

Answers

1. Green Bay, Wisconsin
2. West High School
3. By palming the ball instead of using the laces he improved his distance and accuracy.
4. He sold game programs.
5. Wisconsin
6. Regis College
7. He wasn't. The draft didn't exist yet, and even if it had he probably wouldn't have been selected.
8. He was a handyman.
9. Curly Lambeau gave him a tryout and he joined the team in 1930.
10. $75 a game
11. Tailback, but with Green Bay using the Notre Dame box formation he threw more often than usual.
12. True, for the team's third straight championship.
13. Passing
14. Have a 1,000-yard passing season, when he threw for 1,239 yards in 1936.
15. Don Hutson
16. Cecil Isbell
17. He retired, in part because Isbell was getting more playing time.
18. With the league depleted of talent during World War II, he came out of retirement.
19. The New York Giants
20. The Green Bay Packers
21. Four

Clarke Hinkle

1. True or false? Clarke Hinkle was born in Canada.
2. Where did he play college football?
3. True or false? He's the only player from that school to be inducted into the College Football Hall of Fame.
4. What was his nickname in college?
5. What number did he wear in college?
6. Who said of him, "Without a doubt, the greatest defensive back I have ever seen or coached."
7. True or false? He led his college team to the 1931 national championship.
8. During his pro career, how many receivers did Hinkle say got behind him?
9. What two every-down positions did he play?
10. What positions did he also play?
11. True or false? During his 10 years with the Packers, Hinkle was named first- or second-team all-league each year.
12. True or false? At the time of his retirement in 1941, he was the NFL's all-time leading rusher.
13. Who had held the mark?
14. In what did he lead the league during the 1938 season?
15. Who did he have a personal rivalry with?
16. Who weighed more?
17. What was the outcome of one of their collisions near the sideline in 1934?
18. Who said of him, "They said I was hard to tackle, but here was a guy who didn't have too much trouble."
19. How many points did Hinkle score during his career?
20. Where is Clark Hinkle Field located?

Answers

1. False, he was born in Toronto, Ohio, on April 10, 1909.
2. Bucknell
3. False, Andy "Polyphemus" Wyant began playing for Bucknell in 1887 while still a student at Bucknell Prep. Nicknamed after the Cyclops of Greek mythology, he went on to earn five degrees including Doctor of Medicine.
4. The Lackawanna Express
5. No. 77
6. Hinkle's coach at Bucknell, Carl Snavely.
7. False, but it do go undefeated.
8. One
9. Fullback and linebacker
10. Kicker and punter
11. True
12. True
13. Cliff Battles, with 3,511 yards
14. Scoring
15. Bronko Nagurski
16. Bronko Nagurski had 30 pounds on the 5'11", 202 pound Hinkle.
17. Bronko Nagurski sustained a broken nose and rib fracture.
18. Bronko Nagurski
19. 379
20. It's the Packers' practice field across the street from Lambeau Field.

Paul Hornung

1. When was Paul Hornung born?
2. What's his middle name?
3. Where did he attend high school?
4. Which prominent head coach did he turn down to attend Notre Dame?
5. Name five categories in which Hornung led his team during the 1956 season.
6. Why was his Heisman Trophy so controversial?
7. Who finished second, who had more first-place votes, and which two players also won a region in the voting?
8. What sport did he also play in his sophomore year at Notre Dame?
9. During the 1957 College All-Star Game against the New York Giants, who did Horning race 100 yards against for fun? (Bonus: Name the winner.)
10. What position did Hornung play in his first couple of years with the Packers?
11. What position did Vince Lombardi move him to?
12. In 1959, what statistical category did he lead the NFL in for the first of three years?
13. How long did it take someone to break his single-season scoring record of 176 points, set in 1960?
14. What scoring record did Hornung set in 1961?
15. What major off-field event affected Hornung in 1961?
16. In what two years was he named the NFL's MVP?
17. What honor led to a tax dispute?
18. Why is Hornung listed as playing for the Packers from 1957–1962 and 1964–1966?
19. True or false? Paul Hornung was MVP of Super Bowl I.
20. What team took in him in an expansion draft?

Answers

1. December 23, 1935, in Louisville, Kentucky.
2. Vernon
3. Bishop Benedict Joseph Flaget High School
4. Paul W. "Bear" Bryant, who at the time coached Kentucky.
5. In 1956, he led his team in passing, rushing, scoring, passes broken up, kickoff and punt returns, and punting. He was second in interceptions and tackles.
6. He's the only winner from a losing team, as Notre Dame went 2–8 that season.
7. Tennessee's John Majors was second, Oklahoma's Tom McDonald had more first-place votes, while John Brodie of Stanford and Jim Brown of Syracuse topped voting in their regions.
8. Basketball
9. Abe Woodson. Hornung won by five yards.
10. It's a bit of a trick question because he split time between fullback and quarterback.
11. Tailback
12. Scoring
13. 2006, when San Diego Chargers running back LaDainian Tomlinson scored his 30th touchdown with two games to play. However, Hornung claims that his record should still stand because he did it in 12 games and the NFL should use a points-per-game average.
14. Most points in an NFL championship game.
15. He was called into active service with the Army, but was able to obtain passes to play on Sundays and for the NFL championship game against the New York Giants.
16. 1960 and 1961
17. For being named MVP of the 1961 NFL championship game *Sport* magazine awarded Hornung a 1962 Corvette, which he didn't claim on his tax returns. The matter went to court, where it was ruled that athletes had to include awards in their gross income.
18. He and Alex Karras of the Detroit Lions were suspended for the 1963 season for betting on NFL games and associating with undesirable persons. Both were reinstated for the 1964 season.
19. False. He was the only Packer not to play, due to a pinched nerve.
20. The New Orleans Saints, but he retired during the preseason due to a neck injury.

Robert "Cal" Hubbard

1. Where was Robert Calvin Hubbard born?
2. What two colleges did he play for?
3. Why did he switch?
4. True or false? He's the only representative of either school in the College Football Hall of Fame.
5. Hubbard was considered huge when he played in the 1920s and '30s. How big was he?
6. With which team did he start his professional career?
7. How much was he paid?
8. Because the team was already set at tackle, what positions did he switch to?
9. After two years, winning an NFL title and being named all-league, why did Hubbard request a trade to Green Bay?
10. At which position was he named All-NFL before becoming a staple at tackle with the Packers?
11. True or false? Hubbard wore five different numbers during his six seasons with the Packers.
12. After retiring as a player in 1933, what did he do the following season?
13. Which team persuaded him to come out of retirement and play in 1935?
14. With which team did he start the 1936 season?
15. With which team did he finish his career?
16. In 1969, what honor was bestowed on Hubbard?
17. What second career in sports did he start near the end of his NFL career?
18. Why did he eventually have to retire from the playing fields?
19. True or false? Hubbard is the only person enshrined in both the Pro Football Hall of Fame and Baseball Hall of Fame.
20. Where is Hubbard buried?

Answers

1. Keyesville, Missouri, on October 31, 1900.
2. Centenary College in Louisiana and Geneva College in Pennsylvania.
3. He followed coach Bo McMillin.
4. False. Geneva halfback Joe Thompson is also in the Hall, along with one-time Centenary coach Homer Norton.
5. 6'2", 250 pounds
6. The New York Giants
7. $150 per game
8. End on offense and linebacker on defense.
9. Hubbard didn't like big cities and wasn't comfortable in New York. After a road game in Green Bay he requested the trade or said he would otherwise retire.
10. Guard
11. True. He wore No. 39 in 1929, 40 in 1930 and 1932, 38 in 1931, 27 in 1933, and 51 in 1935.
12. Hubbard was the offensive line coach at Texas A&M.
13. The Green Bay Packers
14. The New York Giants
15. The Pittsburgh Pirates
16. He was voted the greatest tackle of the NFL's first 50 years.
17. Umpiring. He's credited with creating modern positioning in umpiring, with each having specific responsibilities.
18. A hunting accident in 1951 damaged his right eye. However, he was subsequently named MLB's American League supervisor of umpires.
19. True
20. Milan, Missouri

Don Hutson

1. Where was Don Hutson born on January 31, 1913?
2. Where did he play college football?
3. True or false? Hutson holds most of that school's receiving records.
4. What two other sports did he play in college?
5. True or false? Huston had flat feet.
6. While Hutson played end on one side of the offense, who was on the other?
7. Why was it that many NFL teams didn't consider him to be a prize prospect?
8. What was the controversy regarding Hutson signing with the Packers?
9. What did Hutson do on his first play as a pro?
10. Why was Hutson considered by many to be the first modern receiver?
11. What was he the first player in NFL history to do, in 1941?
12. What was he the first player in NFL history to do, in 1942?
13. Consequently, what award did he land both years?
14. During his 11-year career, how many times was he named All-Pro?
15. How many times did he lead the league in receptions?
16. How many times did he lead the league in scoring?
17. True or false? When Hutson retired with 488 pass receptions, he had over 200 more than the next-best player.
18. When he retired, how many NFL records did he hold?
19. Who broke his career record of 99 touchdown receptions? (Hint: It was four decades later.)
20. Why was it controversial?
21. What other positions did he play?
22. How many interceptions did he make?
23. What Hutson record may never be broken?
24. After retiring, what did he do from 1944–1948?
25. Where is the Don Hutson Center?

Answers

1. Pine Bluff, Arkansas
2. Alabama
3. False, but the combination of Dixie Howell to Hutson led the Crimson Tide to a national championship.
4. Track and baseball. He was once timed running the 100-yard dash in 9.8 seconds, and on one occasion ran a track meet and played in a baseball game on the same day.
5. True. Trainers had to tape his feet a special way, which gave him an unusual running motion.
6. Paul W. "Bear" Bryant
7. At 6'1", 182 pounds, many thought he wouldn't survive the rigors of the NFL.
8. He also signed with the Brooklyn Dodgers, but NFL president Joe Carr ruled that the deal with the earliest postmark would be honored. The Packers' contract was postmarked 8:30 AM, 17 minutes earlier than the Dodgers' deal.
9. He scored an 83-yard touchdown pass from Arnie Herber.
10. Because he created many of the pass routes now used in the NFL, including Z-outs, buttonhooks, and hook-and-gos.
11. He became the first player to catch more than 50 passes in a season.
12. He because the first player to have a 1,000-yard receiving season.
13. NFL MVP
14. Nine
15. Eight
16. Five
17. True
18. 18
19. Steve Largent
20. Three of Largent's 100 touchdown catches were against replacement players.
21. Kicker and safety
22. 30
23. In one quarter of a 1945 game, he caught four touchdown passes and kicked five extra points for 29 points.
24. He was a Green Bay assistant coach.
25. It's the Packers' indoor practice facility, located across the street from Lambeau Field.

Henry Jordan

1. Where was Henry Jordan born?
2. Which high school did he attend?
3. For which college football team was he the team captain?
4. In what other sport was he nearly an NCAA champion?
5. True or false? He's enshrined in the College Football Hall of Fame.
6. Which team selected Henry in the 1957 NFL draft?
7. In what round?
8. How did he join the Packers?
9. How many times was he named All-NFL?
10. Which number was greater: times playing in a Pro Bowl or NFL title game?
11. How many games did he miss during his first 12 seasons?
12. How many fumble recoveries did he have?
13. Which number was greater: touchdowns scored or interceptions?
14. Against which team did he score?
15. In the process, what team record did he set?
16. Who eventually broke it?
17. How many defensive teammates from Green Bay were elected to the Pro Football Hall of Fame before Jordan?
18. After he retired, what Wisconsin "Big Gig" was Jordan a part of?
19. What was his title?
20. How old was Jordan when he died in 1977?

Answers

1. Emporia, Virginia, on January 26, 1935.
2. Warwick High School in Newport News, Virginia.
3. Virginia
4. Wrestling. He was the heavyweight runner-up in 1957 NCAA championships.
5. False
6. The Cleveland Browns
7. The fifth round
8. He was traded in exchange for a fourth-round draft choice.
9. Five
10. He played in four Pro Bowls and seven NFL title games.
11. Two
12. 21
13. Actually, he had one of both.
14. The Dallas Cowboys in 1964.
15. Longest fumble return for a touchdown, 60 yards.
16. George Cumby, with his 68-yard fumble return in 1981.
17. Four: Willie Davis, Ray Nitschke, Herb Adderley, and Willie Wood.
18. The massive Milwaukee musical festival called Summerfest.
19. Executive director
20. 42

Earl "Curly" Lambeau

1. Where was Curly Lambeau born on April 9, 1898?
2. From where had his family immigrated?
3. Where was he captain of the high school football team?
4. Which coach did he briefly play for in college?
5. True or false? He made the varsity squad as a freshman.
6. What position did he play?
7. What caused him to leave Notre Dame before his sophomore year?
8. Back home, with what company did he land a job?
9. Why was that important in the history of the Packers?
10. When Lambeau had to raise $250 to re-obtain the Packers' franchise rights in 1922, and basically save the team, how much of his own money did he chip in?
11. True or false? In addition to being a co-founder, Lambeau was essentially the Packers' first quarterback.
12. How many years did he play for the Packers?
13. What was his coaching record with the Packers before the team joined the NFL?
14. How many NFL championships did he win with the Packers?
15. Who won the same number of titles?
16. What was significant about Lambeau's purchase of Rockwood Lodge in 1946?
17. What two other NFL teams did he coach?
18. How many NFL games did he win during his 33-year coaching career?
19. How many games did he win coaching the Packers?
20. Where did Lambeau die while visiting a friend?
21. When was the Packers' stadium renamed Lambeau Field?

Answers

1. Green Bay, Wisconsin
2. Belgium
3. East High School
4. Knute Rockne
5. True
6. Fullback
7. He returned home due to a severe case of tonsillitis.
8. He was a shipping clerk for the Indian Packing Company, making $250 a month.
9. The Indian Packing Company was the initial sponsor of the team.
10. $50
11. True, although he was technically a halfback who took the snap from center (a common practice during that period).
12. 11, from 1919–1929.
13. 19–2–1
14. Six
15. Rival George Halas of the Chicago Bears
16. It provided the Packers with the NFL's first self-contained training facility.
17. The Chicago Cardinals (1950–1951) and Washington Redskins (1952–1953)
18. 229, compared to 134 losses and 22 ties.
19. 209
20. Sturgeon Bay, Wisconsin
21. September 11, 1965

James Lofton

1. Where was James Lofton born on July 5, 1956?
2. Where did he play high school football?
3. What positions did he play?
4. Where did he play college football?
5. In what sport was he an NCAA champion in 1978?
6. True or false? Lofton was a first-team All-American.
7. True or false? As a senior, Lofton had a 1,000-yard season.
8. With what overall pick was Lofton taken in the 1978 draft?
9. How many teams did Lofton play for?
10. After being named to the Pro Bowl seven times with the Packers, with which team did he make his final appearance?
11. How many times was Lofton named All-Pro?
12. How many seasons did he play?
13. True or false? Lofton was the first Packers player to enter the Pro Football Hall of Fame without a tie to either Curly Lambeau or Vince Lombardi.
14. True or false? Lofton holds the NFL's career record for receiving yards, with 14,004.
15. True or false? Lofton was the first NFL player to score a touchdown in the 1970s, '80s, and '90s.
16. In 1991, Lofton became the second-oldest player to record 200-plus all-purpose yards in an NFL game. Who was the oldest?
17. After his playing days concluded, which with two teams did he serve as an assistant coach?

Answers

1. Fort Ord, California
2. George Washington High School in Los Angeles.
3. Quarterback and safety
4. Stanford
5. Long jump, with a wind-aided leap of 26 feet, 11¾ inches.
6. False, he was second-team.
7. True, he had 1,010 yards on 57 catches.
8. Sixth
9. Five: Green Bay Packers,1978–1986; Los Angeles Raiders, 1987–1988; Buffalo Bills; 1989–1992; Philadelphia Eagles, 1993.
10. The Buffalo Bills in 1991.
11. Four
12. 16
13. True
14. False, it was a record when he retired but has since been surpassed.
15. True
16. Mel Gray was 35 years, 204 days old when he did it; Lofton was 35 years, 108 days.
17. San Diego Chargers and Oakland Raiders

Vince Lombardi

1.   When and where was Vince Lombardi born?
2.   Before he got into football, what was he on the path to become?
3.   Where did Lombardi play high school football?
4.   Where did he play college football?
5.   Who was his coach?
6.   Despite his size, what position did Lombardi play?
7.   What was the nickname of the unit he played on?
8.   What did Lombardi call the most "devastating loss of my life"?
9.   Before he gave coaching a shot, what did he spend a semester studying?
10. With what prominent college program was he an assistant coach for five years before turning to the NFL?
11. When he was essentially the offensive coordinator of the New York Giants, who was their defensive coordinator?
12. What did Lombardi fear might cost him a chance to become a head coach?
13. How old was Lombardi when he became an NFL head coach?
14. Was that his first head coaching job?
15. True or false? Lombardi was named Coach of the Year after his first season with the Packers.
16. What job was he offered after his second season with the Packers?
17. Who later asked him to coach at Army?
18. What was the only loss Lombardi experienced in an NFL championship game?
19. Who eventually topped Lombardi's streak of nine-straight postseason wins?
20. What trademark play did Lombardi design in which Paul Hornung (or others) would "run to daylight"?
21. How many losing seasons had Washington endured before Lombardi took over?
22. Where is Lombardi Square?
23. On what day did Lombardi die, and how old was he?

Answers

1. June 1, 1913, in Brooklyn, New York.
2. A Catholic priest
3. St. Francis Prep
4. Fordham
5. Jim Crowley, one of the Four Horsemen at Notre Dame
6. At 5'8", 183 pounds, he was an offensive lineman
7. The Seven Blocks of Granite
8. A 7–6 loss to NYU the final game of his senior season, costing the team a chance to play in the Rose Bowl.
9. Law
10. Army, under head coach Red Blaik.
11. Tom Landry
12. Prejudice against his Italian heritage
13. 45
14. No, he was the head coach at St. Cecilia High School.
15. True
16. The head coaching job with the New York Giants.
17. President John F. Kennedy
18. The 1960 NFL title game against Philadelphia.
19. Bill Belichick, who won 10 in a row from 2002–2006.
20. The Lombardi sweep or the Packer power sweep
21. 14, which he snapped with a 7–5–2 record.
22. Brooklyn, New York
23. September 3, 1970, at age 57.

John "Blood" McNally

1. Where was Johnny "Blood" McNally born?
2. How old was he when he graduated from high school?
3. Where did he attend college?
4. Who came up with the nickname "Blood"?
5. Why did he need the alias Johnny Blood?
6. What position did he play?
7. What jersey numbers did he wear for the Packers?
8. In what off-field category did he lead the league?
9. In addition to two stints with the Packers from 1929–1933 and 1935–1936, which four teams did he play for?
10. What was he known as with his first team?
11. How many titles did he win with the Packers?
12. What did he do on his first play with the Steelers?
13. How many NFL touchdowns did he score?
14. What did McNally take the day off from coaching his minor-league team, the Kenosha Cardinals, to do?

Johnny "Blood" McNally

15. From 1950–1952, where did McNally coach?

16. What did he tell the incoming coach upon leaving with a 13–9 record?

17. Who was that coach?

18. What did McNally do during World War II?

19. Who said of McNally, "Even when Johnny does the expected, he does it in an unexpected way."?

20. What movie character is based on McNally, who played him, and what's the name of the movie?

Answers

1. New Richmond, Wisconsin, on November 27, 1903.

2. 14

3. St. John's University in Collegeville, Minnesota

4. He did. While passing by a movie theater, McNally saw the title of the film *Blood and Sand* on the marquee. He turned to his friend and said, "That's it. You be Sand. I'll be Blood."

5. McNally had a year of college eligibility, so used the name to play pro football without losing it.

6. Halfback

7. No. 24, 1929–1930; No. 20, 1931–1932; No. 14, 1933; No. 26, 1935; No. 55, 1936

8. Times fined

9. 1925–1926, Milwaukee Badgers; 1926–1927, Duluth Eskimos; 1928, Pottsville Maroons; 1934, 1937–1938, Pittsburgh Pirates

10. The "Vagabond Halfback" for his spontaneity and off-field behavior.

11. Four

12. He ran back a kick 92 yards for a touchdown.

13. 49

14. McNally played one final game with the Buffalo Tigers of the American Football League.

15. His alma mater, St. John's.

16. "Nobody can win at St. John's."

17. John Gagliardi, who through 2010 had won 454 games, more than any other coach in college football history.

18. He served as a cryptographer in India.

19. His wife, Marguerite, whom he married in his mid-forties.

20. Dodge Connolly, played by George Clooney in *Leatherheads*.

Mike Michalske

1. Where was Mike Michalske born?
2. What's his real first name?
3. Where was he an All-American in college?
4. What position did he play?
5. With which NFL team he play his rookie season?
6. What happened to that franchise?
7. How did he join the Packers?
8. Which two future Hall of Fame players also joined the Packers in 1929?
9. How did he end up playing guard?
10. What nickname did he earn with the Packers?
11. Why?
12. What was he known for doing on defense?
13. Out of 104 games during his years with the Packers, how many games did he miss?
14. With what ailment did he play most of his career?
15. How many times was he a consensus All-Pro?
16. What did Michalske spend the 1936 season doing?
17. What injury caused him to retire for good after the 1937 season?
18. True or false? He was the first guard inducted into the Pro Football Hall of Fame.
19. Which former player named Michalske to his all-time team?
20. After his playing career ended, at what college was Michalske the head coach from 1942–1946?

Answers

1. Cleveland, Ohio, on April 24, 1903.
2. August. Mike is his middle name.
3. Penn State
4. Fullback—but he also played some at guard, end, and tackle.
5. Red Grange's New York Yankees of the American Football League.
6. It disbanded.
7. Michalske turned down the $400 salary due him so he could be a free agent.
8. Cal Hubbard and Johnny "Blood" McNally
9. Michalske talked Curly Lambeau into trying him on the line.
10. Iron Mike
11. He also played on the defensive line, so he essentially played the full 60 minutes of a game.
12. Blitzing
13. Nine, five of which were during his final season.
14. An unrepaired congenital abdominal hernia.
15. Six, but he was also once a non-consensus selection.
16. He was an assistant football coach under Ernie Nevers and the head basketball coach at Lafayette College.
17. He sustained a back injury.
18. True
19. New York Giants quarterback Benny Friedman, who described him as "a quarterback-playing guard."
20. Iowa State

Ray Nitschke

1. What's his full name?
2. Where was Ray Nitschke born?
3. Who raised him after both parents died?
4. What position did he play at Proviso East High School?
5. Where did he play college football?
6. What offensive position did he switch to his sophomore year?
7. How many touchdowns did he score against Iowa State?
8. True or false? Nitschke is in the College Football Hall of Fame.
9. In what round of the 1958 draft was he selected?
10. How old was Nitschke at the time?
11. True or false? Nitschke immediately became the starter once Vince Lombardi was hired following the 1958 season.
12. What did he do to be named the MVP of the 1962 NFL championship game?
13. In which Super Bowl—I or II—did he have more tackles?
14. Where was Nitschke's last regular-season game played?
15. How did the Packers honor him in the final seconds?
16. How many interceptions did he make during his career?
17. True or false? Nitschke was the first Green Bay defender from the dynasty years inducted into the Hall of Fame.
18. Where did he die in 1998?
19. True or false? A metal tower on the Packers practice field once fell on Nitschke.
20. Where is Ray Nitschke Field?

Nitschke stares down the offense just before the snap. *(Getty Images)*

Answers

1. Raymond Ernest Nitschke
2. Elmwood Park, Illinois, on December 29, 1936.
3. An older brother. Their father died when Ray was three, and his mother when he was 13.
4. Quarterback
5. Illinois
6. Fullback
7. Four
8. False
9. Third
10. 20
11. False, he didn't become a full-time starter until 1962.
12. He recovered two fumbles and deflected a pass that was intercepted.
13. Nitschke had six tackles in Super Bowl I, nine in Super Bowl II.
14. Tulane Stadium to face the 1–11–1 Saints.
15. They threw him a pass for his only career reception. He received a standing ovation and the Saints refused to tackle him, forcing him out of bounds after a 34-yard gain.
16. 25
17. True
18. Venice, Florida, en route to his winter home in Naples. Nitschke was 61.
19. True. He wasn't hurt but it drove a spike into his helmet.
20. It's one of Green Bay's two outdoor practice fields across the street from Lambeau Stadium.

Jim Ringo

1. Where was Jim Ringo born?
2. Where did he attend high school?
3. Where did he play college football?
4. What was the outcome of his final collegiate game?
5. In what round did the Packers draft him in 1953?
6. What heavily influenced his draft position?
7. How old was Ringo when he was drafted?
8. True or false? At one point during his rookie training camp, Ringo quit the team.
9. Who was coaching the Packers at that time?
10. What was his highest weight as a player?
11. True or false? Ringo wasn't named to the Pro Bowl until after Vince Lombardi arrived.
12. How many consecutive games did he play for the Packers?
13. To which team was he traded after the 1963 season?
14. How many career rushing yards did Ringo have?
15. Name the five NFL teams he served as an assistant coach (two teams twice).
16. Which unit did he create with the Bills to help running back O.J. Simpson?
17. What was Ringo's coaching record during two seasons with the Buffalo Bills?

Answers

1. Orange, New Jersey
2. Phillipsburg High School
3. Syracuse
4. His team was pounded by Alabama in the Orange Bowl, 61–5.
5. Seventh
6. At 6'2", 211 pounds, he was considered vastly undersized.
7. 20
8. True
9. Gene Ronzani
10. 235
11. False; he was named to the Pro Bowl and All-Pro for the first time in 1957.
12. 126
13. The Philadelphia Eagles
14. 13
15. The Rams, Bills, Bears, Patriots, and Jets
16. The offensive line known as "the Electric Company."
17. 3–20

Bart Starr

1. What's his full name?
2. When and where was Bart Starr born?
3. How did his younger brother die in 1947?
4. Where did Starr attend high school?
5. What happened when Starr tried out for football?
6. True or false? After receiving numerous scholarship options Starr chose to play for Paul W. "Bear" Bryant.
7. True or false? Starr played sparingly his senior season at Alabama.
8. Who recommended Starr to the Packers?
9. In 1956, what round of the draft did the Packers select Starr?
10. Who did Vince Lombardi pull to insert Starr as starting quarterback?
11. From 1960–1967, how many games did Starr win?
12. In 10 career playoff games, how many did he lose?
13. How many times did Starr attempt 300 or more passes in a season?
14. How many times did he lead the league in passing?
15. When he retired as a player, who was the only quarterback to have a better career passer rating than Starr's 80.5?
16. Who had a better career completion percentage than Starr's 57.4?
17. Who hired Starr to be the Packers' quarterbacks coach?
18. How many playoff appearances did Starr have as a head coach?
19. To whom does the annual Bart Starr Award go each year?

Answers

1. Bryan Bartlett Starr
2. January 9, 1934, in Montgomery, Alabama.
3. He stepped on a dog bone while playing in the yard and died from tetanus three days later.
4. Sidney Lanier High School
5. He quit after two weeks, only to return after his father gave him the option of playing football or working in the family garden.
6. False. At the time Bryant was at Kentucky, and despite offering a scholarship, Starr elected to attend Alabama to be closer to his girlfriend who was planning to attend Auburn. (They eventually eloped.)
7. True. Starr was coming off a back injury and Coach J.B. Whitworth had started a youth movement.
8. Alabama basketball coach Johnny Dees, who was friends with Packers personnel director Jack Vainisi.
9. 17th, No. 199 overall.
10. Lamar McHan
11. 62, compared to 24 losses and four ties. The Packers won six division and five NFL titles, and the first two Super Bowls.
12. One
13. Zero
14. Three
15. Otto Graham at 86.6.
16. No one
17. Dan Devine, who he later replaced as head coach.
18. One
19. An NFL player of outstanding character.

Jim Taylor

1. Where was Taylor born on September 20, 1935?
2. Not surprisingly, where did he play college football?
3. Where did attend college first?
4. Taylor's final collegiate game against Tulane started what impressive streak?
5. What was he the first NFL running back to do?
6. When he had 35 carries against the New York Giants in the 1962 NFL championship game, what record did he set?
7. What year did he win the NFL rushing title?
8. True or false? He's the only player in Packers history to lead the league in rushing.
9. How many rushing yards did he have that season?
10. How many rushing touchdowns did he have that season?
11. Who eventually broke his team record for rushing yards?
12. True or false? Taylor finished his career with more than 10,000 net yards rushing and receiving.
13. How many times did Taylor have at least 100 receiving yards?
14. In the 2,173 times he handled the ball, how many times did Taylor fumble?
15. Although they had different styles, to whom was Taylor frequently compared?
16. True or false? When he retired, Taylor's 83 rushing touchdowns were a league record.
17. With which team did he play his final season?
18. How many rushing yards did he have that season?
19. How many Super Bowls did he win?
20. Until what year was Taylor listed among the league's top-20 career rushing leaders?

Answers

1. Baton Rouge, Louisiana
2. LSU
3. Hinds Junior College
4. A 22-game unbeaten streak
5. He was the first to have five straight 1,000-yard seasons.
6. Most carries in an NFL title game.
7. 1962
8. True
9. 1,474
10. 19
11. Ahman Green. He broke his single-season mark in 2003, and his career record in 2009.
12. True, 10,539
13. Seven, six of them with the Packers.
14. 34
15. Jim Brown
16. False, but he trailed only Jim Brown, who had 106.
17. The New Orleans Saints
18. 390 yards on 130 carries and two touchdowns for the expansion team.
19. One
20. 2003

Vince Lombardi congratulates Jim Taylor on winning the 1962 MVP Award.

Reggie White

1. What's his full name?
2. Where was Reggie White born on December 19, 1961?
3. At what age did he become an ordained minister?
4. Where did he play college football?
5. Which school records did he set in sacks: game, season, or career?
6. True or false? He won the Lombardi Award as college football's best lineman.
7. With which team did White sign out of college?
8. In two seasons with that team, how many sacks did he record?
9. What did he do in his NFL debut?
10. True or false? During his rookie season White was named the NFL's Defensive Player of the Year.
11. When did he win that award?
12. During the strike-shortened 1987 season, how many sacks did White have in 12 games?
13. True or false? During eight seasons with the Philadelphia Eagles he had more sacks than number of games played.
14. Why did White sign a free-agent deal with Green Bay?
15. How many championships did he win?
16. After he initially retired in 1998, who passed him on the NFL's career sacks list?
17. Which team did he come out of retirement to play for in 2000?
18. In how many consecutive seasons did White have at least 10 sacks?
19. To how many consecutive Pro Bowls was he named?
20. From what did White die on December 26, 2004?
21. How old was he?
22. Where is he buried?

Answers

1. Reginald Howard White
2. Chattanooga, Tennessee
3. 17
4. Tennessee
5. All three, with four in a game, 15 in a season, and 32 over his career.
6. False. White was a finalist.
7. The Memphis Showboats of the USFL
8. 23½, to go with 198 tackles and seven forced fumbles.
9. He had 2½ sacks and deflected a pass that was intercepted and returned for a touchdown.
10. False, after notching 13 sacks he was named the NFL's Defensive Rookie of the Year.
11. 1998
12. 20, averaging 1.75 per game.
13. True. 124 sacks in 121 games played.
14. He said that God told him to.
15. Just one, the victory in Super Bowl XXXI.
16. Bruce Smith
17. The Carolina Panthers
18. Nine
19. 13
20. Cardiac arrhythmia
21. 43
22. Glenwood Memorial Park in Mooresville, North Carolina.

Willie Wood

1. What is Willie Wood's middle name?
2. Where was he born on December 23, 1936?
3. Where did he play college football?
4. What distinction did he achieve there?
5. Which NFL team selected Wood in the 1960 draft?
6. What did Wood do to keep his football hopes alive?
7. To what position did the Packers move him?
8. How long did it take for him to become a starter?

9. How many times was he named All-Pro?

10. How many championship games did he play?

11. How many career interceptions did he have?

12. True or false? Wood never led the NFL in interceptions.

13. In which other category did he lead the league in 1961?

14. True or false? During his 12-year career he eclipsed 1,000 yards on punt returns.

15. Which number is greater: interception returns for touchdowns or punt returns for touchdowns?

16. Who eventually broke his NFL record for consecutive starts by a defensive back, with 154?

17. Including Wood, how many undrafted free agents have gone on to be enshrined in the Pro Football Hall of Fame?

18. Which two teams did he serve as head coach of, and in the process became each league's first black head coach?

Answers

1. Vernell
2. Washington D.C.
3. The University of Southern California
4. Wood was the first black quarterback in the Pac-10 conference.
5. No team took him.
6. He sent postcards to teams asking for a tryout.
7. Free safety
8. Just his second season
9. Nine
10. Six
11. 48
12. False. He led the league with nine in 1962.
13. Punt returns, averaging 16.1 yards.
14. True. He had 187 returns for 1,391 yards.
15. He had two of each.
16. Ronde Barber
17. 13
18. The Philadelphia Bell of the World Football League and the Toronto Argonauts of the Canadian Football League.

Twelve

The Ice Bowl

In 2002, the 35th anniversary of the Ice Bowl was fast approaching and the decision was made at my newspaper to commemorate it in some way that hadn't been done before. So in conjunction with our team coverage we asked any readers who had attended the game to please contact yours truly.

Naturally, my mailbox overflowed and I received more emails than I could count. One person swore he had Don Meredith's jacket from the game and that it was hanging on the wall of his basement. Naturally, that got my attention—and sure enough it looked exactly like what the Dallas Cowboys were wearing that day, complete with the team name across the front.

Back then security wasn't nearly as intense as it now, and fans being on the field both during and after games wasn't unusual. Considering the weather conditions it was probably even more lax than normal, so the notion that this particular person jumped the fence to get warm at a fire by the Cowboys bench and no one said anything was more than plausible.

So is the possibility that he picked up Meredith's coat when the quarterback entered the game at some point, put it on, and with the temperature continuing to drop was able to tuck it under his arm and leave with it.

When I called the Dallas Cowboys to try and confirm any part of the story, obviously there was no way to do so. However, I'll never forget what the team official told me before we got off the phone: "If it was Meredith's jacket you can be damn sure they found him another one."

Nevertheless, the most famous game in Green Bay Packers history isn't a Super Bowl, but one played for the right to get there.

Quiz!

1. When was the Ice Bowl played?
2. What was the temperature at game time?
3. What was the wind chill estimated to be?
4. True or false? The field's heating system didn't work.
5. What was the only heated place fans could go to in the stadium?
6. What was the announced attendance?
7. What was the final score?
8. Who caught two touchdown passes to help Green Bay take a 14–0 lead?
9. Who scored on a seven-yard fumble return for the Cowboys?
10. Who threw a 50-yard touchdown pass to wide receiver Lance Rentzel for the Cowboys?
11. With the game on the line in the final moments, who was stopped twice at the 1-yard line?
12. On third-and-goal with 16 seconds remaining, who wanted to call for a quarterback sneak?
13. Who said, "Well, run it and let's get the hell out of here."
14. How many timeouts did Green Bay have remaining when it ran the play?

15. Who did Starr run behind to dive into the end zone?

16. Who thought he was getting the ball?

17. Why did he put his hands up in the air?

18. What was the difference in total yards between the teams?

19. Who passed for more yards: Bart Starr or Don Meredith?

20. Who said of the team's trip home to Dallas, "Not one word was spoken the entire flight."

21. How may future Hall of Famers were involved in the game? (Hint: Make sure to count the non-players.)

Answers

1. December 31, 1967
2. –13 degrees
3. –40 degrees
4. True. At first some of the Cowboys believed that it was off intentionally.
5. The bathrooms
6. 50,861
7. Green Bay won 21–17.
8. Boyd Dowler
9. George Andrie
10. Dan Reeves
11. Running back Donny Anderson
12. Bart Starr
13. Vince Lombardi
14. Zero
15. Guard Jerry Kramer and center Ken Bowman
16. Chuck Mercein
17. Not to signal touchdown, but to show officials he wasn't pushing Starr into the end zone, which would have resulted in a penalty.
18. Three. Green Bay had the slight edge, 195–192.
19. Starr, by a wide margin, 191–59.
20. Cowboys receiver Lance Rentzel
21. 14. For the Cowboys: Tex Schramm, Tom Landry, Bob Lilly, Mel Renfro, Rayfield Wright, and Bob Hayes. For the Packers: Vince Lombardi, Bart Starr, Forrest Gregg, Willie Davis, Ray Nitschke, Henry Jordan, and Herb Adderley.

Thirteen

Miscellaneous

From the stadiums to the Super Bowls and the Hall of Famers, just about every aspect of the Green Bay Packers has been covered, right?

Hardly.

This section will test your knowledge of oddities and eccentricities. We'll look at the one-hit wonders, the great moments, and the forgotten stories of Packers lore.

What professional wrestler was on the '82 team? What is a "Bay of Pigs" game? Who were "the Three Amigos"? What famous Packers kick led the NFL to raise the height of the goalposts?

From the Bobby Dillon's glass eye to Dominic Olejniczak's warning to Aaron Rodgers right arm; Clarke Hinkle, Kitrick Taylor, the highest scoring game in *MNF* history, and Lambeau Field's place in the top 20 sports venues of the 20th Century (according to one magazine at least), this chapter revels in the absurd and unbelievable.

 **Quiz!**

1. True or false? Vince Lombardi said, "Winning isn't everything"?
2. Which future famous wrestler spent the 1982 season on the Packers' injured reserve list?
3. When the Packers play in a "Bay of Pigs" game, which team are they facing?
4. Whose creed was, "Get to the Bronk before he gets to me"?
5. What's the second-coldest game in Packers history?
6. Which team(s) did Green Bay defeat 15 straight times?
7. To which opponent(s) did the Packers lose 11 straight times?
8. Who holds the Green Bay record for special-teams tackles in a single season?
9. True or false? George Halas once borrowed $1,500 from the Packers to meet his payroll for the Chicago Bears.
10. Which team did Green Bay defeat 48–47 in the highest scoring game on *Monday Night Football*?
11. How was the game decided?
12. What's the NFL record for times carrying a coach off the field?
13. Who did Green Bay sign as an undrafted free agent in 1994, after he played college football at Northern Iowa?
14. Who told Packers president Dominic Olejniczak in 1959 that if he hired Vince Lombardi as head coach his own team would be in trouble?
15. What was Vince Lombardi's record against that person's team?
16. When was the last time the Packers led the overall series against the Chicago Bears?
17. What was the first losing season in Packers history?
18. Of the 11 men who served as assistant coaches under Vince Lombardi in Green Bay, how many went on to become head coaches?
19. Name them.
20. True or false? When Phil Bengtson replaced Vince Lombardi that first year, he faced the toughest schedule in Packers history.

21. Through 2009, which school has produced the most Green Bay Packers?
22. Name the next 11 schools in order.
23. What controversial kick led the NFL to raise the height of the goalposts to a minimum of 20 feet above the crossbar?
24. What honor did both Ron Wolf and Ted Thompson receive from the *Sporting News*?
25. How much did it cost to build the Don Hutson Center, which opened in 1994?
26. Which team won the only overtime game between Green Bay and the Chicago Bears?
27. How were the winning points scored?
28. When Brett Favre came off the bench on September 20, 1992, against Cincinnati, by what score were the Packers trailing?
29. What was the final score?
30. Who caught the game-winning touchdown with 13-seconds remaining?
31. What was Green Bay's record in the annual Chicago College All-Star Game?
32. In 1999, when *Sports Illustrated* listed the top 20 sports venues of the 20th century, where did Lambeau Field rank?
33. Name the only venues listed ahead of Lambeau Field.
34. True or false? Aaron Rodgers became the first player in NFL history to have 4,000 passing yards in each of his first three years as a starter.
35. Excluding division teams, which opponent has Green Bay defeated the most at Lambeau Field through 2009?
36. When Bobby Dillon and Irv Comp were setting interception records with the Packers, what did they have in common?
37. Who were known as "the Three Amigos"?
38. Which two players were named to nine Pro Bowls as Packers? (Bonus: Name who had eight.)
39. How many Heisman Trophy winners have played for the Packers?
40. Name them.

Answers

1. False, he actually didn't say it. He said "Winning is not a sometime thing, it's an all the time thing," which was paraphrased down to the more popular, albeit incorrect, quote.
2. Larry Pfohl, otherwise known as Lex Luger, who never played in a game.
3. The Tampa Bay Buccaneers. ESPN broadcaster Chris Berman came up with the nickname.
4. Clarke Hinkle, regarding his legendary rivalry with Bronko Nagurski of the Chicago Bears.
5. It was −1 when Green Bay hosted the New York Giants on January 20, 2008, and lost 23–20.
6. The Chicago Cardinals, from 1937–1946.
7. Both the Detroit Lions (1949–1954) and Los Angeles Rams (1948–1953)
8. John Dorsey, with 35 in 1984.
9. True, it happened during the Great Depression
10. The Washington Redskins in 1983.
11. Washington kicker Mark Mosley missed a last-second field goal.
12. It's believed to be five, the number of times the Packers carried Vince Lombardi off the field, including his first victory as head coach.
13. Kurt Warner, who didn't start in college until his senior year.
14. George Halas
15. Lombardi went 13–5 against the Chicago Bears.
16. 1932, when the Packers had an 11–10–5 edge.
17. 1933, Green Bay's 13th season in the NFL, when it finished 5–7–1.
18. Five
19. Bill Austin (Pittsburgh, Washington), Phil Bengtson (Green Bay), Jerry Burns (Minnesota), Tom Fears (New Orleans), and Norb Hecker (Atlanta)
20. True, based on opponent records at the end of the season.
21. Notre Dame, with 52
22. Minnesota (44), Wisconsin (39), Southern California (33), Nebraska (31), Michigan (28), Alabama and Iowa (tied 25), Ohio State (24), Michigan State (22), and Marquette and Oklahoma (tied 21)
23. Don Chandler's 22-yard controversial field goal to send the 1965 Packers-Colts playoff game into overtime.
24. NFL Executive of the Year
25. $4.7 million
26. The Packers won 12–6 on September 7, 1980.
27. Chester Marcol caught his own blocked kick by Alan Page and ran 25 yards for game-winning touchdown six minutes into overtime.
28. 20–7
29. Green Bay won 24–23.
30. Kitrick Taylor caught the 35-yard touchdown.
31. 6–2
32. Eighth
33. Yankee Stadium, Augusta National, Michie Stadium (West Point), Cameron Indoor Stadium (Duke), Bislett Stadium (Oslo, Norway), Wrigley Field, and Roland Garros (Paris)
34. False. He was the first to do it his first two years starting, but missed in 2010 with 3,922 yards. He was also the first quarterback in league history to throw 30 or more touchdowns, seven or fewer interceptions, and rush for five touchdowns in the same season.

35. The San Francisco 49ers, 11 times with just three losses.
36. Both only had one good eye. Dillon had a glass eye and Comp was blind in one eye.
37. Brett Favre, Mark Chmura, and Frank Winters
38. Forrest Gregg and Brett Favre. Willie Wood was named eight times.
39. Six
40. Year, Name, Pos., School, Years with Packers
1941, Bruce Smith, B, Minnesota, 1945–1948
1956, Paul Hornung, B, Notre Dame, 1957–1962, 1964–1966
1990, Ty Detmer, QB, Brigham Young, 1992–1995
1991, Desmond Howard, WR, Michigan, 1996, 1999
1996, Danny Wuerffel, QB, Florida, 2000
1997, Charles Woodson, CB, Michigan, 2006–2010

Reggie White hugs Brett Favre after winning the NFC Championship game on January 12, 1997.

Fourteen

The Two-Minute Drill

We'll ease you into this.

What was so unusual about the Green Bay Packers' season opener in 2010? To refresh your memory, Green Bay began its Super Bowl drive with a 27–20 victory at Philadelphia, with Aaron Rodgers throwing two touchdown passes and Mason Crosby hitting a team-record 56-yard field goal.

The Packers opened against the Eagles for the sixth time in franchise history, but for the first time in Philadelphia. Green Bay was 4–1 in the previous openers, which were played in 1934, 1940, 1968, 1991, and 2007—when as a rookie, Crosby's 42-yard field goal with two seconds remaining was the difference in the 16–13 victory.

Since 1992, only two seasons didn't include either the Packers or Eagles in the playoffs, 1999 and 2005, and with the win Green Bay won its fourth-straight opener, one of just three teams to do so. The other two were New England and Pittsburgh, which it would eventually beat for the Lombardi Trophy.

But what made the game unusual was simply that Green Bay opened its season away from Lambeau Field. Since 1986, it was just the fourth time in the past 25 years it had done so.

What was Green Bay's record in those four games? 3–1.

Of the three wins, which was the only one that didn't lead to a Super Bowl championship? 2004.

You probably get the idea by now. When it comes to Packers trivia, these are some of the hardest of the hard—ones even the most die-hard fans will struggle with.

1. When Green Bay went on its "Western Tour" after the 1936 season, name the opponents and the five cities in which it played.
2. Of the five games, which drew the most fans?
3. In 1992, when Sterling Sharpe became one of only seven players in NFL history to win the "triple crown" at the receiver position—leading the league in receiving yards, receiving touchdowns, and receptions—who did he join?
4. In 2008, when Brett Favre broke his silence about potentially coming back for another season, who did he do the television interview with and what's his or her connection to Green Bay?
5. There have been five players in history—including one Packer—who were named both the Heisman Trophy winner and NFL's MVP. Name them.
6. What's the name of the fan who attends games dressed up as the Pope? (Note: St. Vince doesn't count.)
7. Who holds the team record for touchdowns by a rookie?
8. Who holds the team record for rushing touchdowns by a rookie?
9. Who has the team record for average gain per rush (at least 750 attempts)?
10. Who has the Packers' record for fair catches?
11. Who once threw six touchdown passes against Green Bay?
12. Who started at quarterback in Green Bay's first league game?
13. Who started at quarterback in the Packers' second game?
14. Who was Curly Lambeau's boss at the Indian Packing Company, which sponsored the team its first season?

15. Who was the chairman of the Acme Packing Company when it backed the team?
16. Which Green Bay Packer is often credited with creating the draw play?
17. Where was he born?
18. Which player listed on the all-time roster was an impostor?
19. As mentioned previously there are 10 pro franchises that have used their nicknames longer than the Packers (1919). Name them.
20. Name the only Green Bay coach who made his Packers debut outside of Wisconsin.
21. Name the three who faced the Chicago Bears in their first game.
22. Which Green Bay Packer was named to a Pro Bowl after being selected in the 20th round of the NFL Draft?
23. Who is the only Packer drafted after pick No. 300 to be named to a Pro Bowl?
24. Name the team's 11 non-drafted free agents named to the Pro Bowl.
25. Name the only team that had a better home record over a 10-year span than Green Bay's 69–11 stretch from 1993–2002.
26. Name Green Bay's first developmental squad in 1989. (Hint: There were four players.)
27. In the 2008 regular-season finale, Ryan Grant and DeShawn Wynn both had 106 rushing yards to become the fifth tandem in Green Bay history have 100-yard performances in the same game. Name the other four.
28. During his sophomore year at Alabama, in which statistical category was Bart Starr second nationally, and who beat him out?
29. Who became the only player in NFL history to record two safeties in a single game when he did it against the Packers?
30. It was previously mentioned that a Green Bay Packer was the league's first 1,000-yard passer in single season. Who was the first 2,000-yard passer?
31. In 1993, when Green Bay drafted Wayne Simmons and George Teague in the first round, who was the only player selected by the Packers to not make the team?

32. In 1965, what overshadowed Paul Hornung's team-record five touchdowns against the Baltimore Colts?

33. Name the 23 people associated with the Green Bay Packers enshrined in the Wisconsin Sports Hall of Fame (through 2009).

34. What weather issue put the team in debt in 1922 and helped lead to the first stock sale?

35. Who caught the game-winning touchdown in the inaugural game at Lambeau Field?

36. Name the 15 Packers who played in the World League. (Bonus: Name the teams for which they played.)

37. True or false? More than 50 Packers played in the USFL.

38. Name them.

39. Name the offensive players on the *Green Bay Press-Gazette*'s All-Century Team.

40. Name the defensive players on the *Green Bay Press-Gazette*'s All-Century Team.

41. Name the special-teams players on the *Green Bay Press-Gazette*'s All-Century Team.

42. Name the coach and player of the century.

10. Willie Wood, with 102 from 1960–1971.
11. Minnesota's Tommy Kramer on September 28, 1986.
12. Adolph Kliebhan, although he wasn't in for long during his only career league game.
13. Art Schmael, after which Curly Lambeau made himself the starting quarterback.
14. Frank Peck
15. John Clair
16. Guard Charles "Buckets" Goldenberg
17. Odessa, Russian Empire, on April 15, 1911.
18. The person claiming to be Jack "Dollie" Gray, an All-American end from Princeton, who played one game in 1923.
19. Cincinnati Reds, baseball, 1878; Pittsburgh Pirates, baseball, 1891; St. Louis Cardinals, baseball, 1900; Detroit Tigers, baseball, 1901; Chicago Cubs, baseball, 1902; Chicago White Sox, baseball, 1904; Boston Red Sox, baseball, 1907; New York Yankees, baseball, 1913; Cleveland Indians, baseball, 1915; Montreal Canadiens, hockey, 1917
20. Out of 14 head coaches, no one's ever done it.
21. Ray "Scooter" McLean (1958), Vince Lombardi (1959), and Mike McCarthy (2006). Only Lombardi won, 9–6.
22. Charles Schulz, 1939
23. Larry McCarren, pick No. 308 in the 12th round of the 1973 draft, who was eventually named to two Pro Bowls (1982–1983).
24. Arnie Herber (1939), Hank Bruder (1939), Milt Gantenbein (1939), Clarke Hinkle (1938–1940), Charles "Buckets" Goldenberg (1939), Joe Laws (1939) Don Hutson (1939–1942), Carl Mulleneaux (1939–1940), Willie Wood (1962, 1964–1967, 1969–1970), Bob Brown (1972), Paul Coffman (1982–1984)
25. From 1967–1976, the Oakland Raiders went 60–8–2 at home.
26. George Cooper, fullback, Ohio State; Mark Hall, defensive end, Southwestern Louisiana; Tim Moore, linebacker, Michigan State; Stan Shiver, safety, Florida State.
27. John Brockington (142) and MacArthur Lane (101), at Chicago, 1973; Eddie Lee Ivery (145) and Gerry Ellis (101), at Minnesota, 1980; Eddie Lee Ivery (109) and Gerry Ellis (101), vs. Tampa Bay, 1985; Ahman Green (106) and Vernand Morency (101), vs. Arizona, 2006
28. Bart Starr's punting average of 41.4 yards per kick ranked second in the nation in 1953 behind Zeke Bratkowski.
29. Fred Dryer of the Los Angeles Rams on October 21, 1973.
30. Cecil Isbell completed 146 of 268 passes for 2,021 yards in 1942.
31. Howard safety Tim Watson
32. Gale Sayers scored six that day against San Francisco.
33. 1951: Don Hutson, end/defensive back; Clarke Hinkle, back
    1955: Howard "Cub" Buck, tackle
    1957: Joseph "Red" Dunn, back
    1960: Johnny "Blood" McNally, back
    1961: Earl "Curly" Lambeau, coach and back
    1967: Lavvie Dilweg, end; Arnie Herber, back; Verne Lewellen, back
    1970: Mike Michalske, guard

1973: Tony Canadeo, back; Charles "Buckets" Goldenberg, guard/back
1976: Vince Lombardi, coach and general manager
1978: Lisle Blackbourn, coach
1981: Ray Nitschke, linebacker; Bart Starr, quarterback
1988: Willie Davis, defensive end
1990: Paul Hornung, back
1993: Jerry Kramer, guard
2001: Jim Taylor, fullback
2003: Fuzzy Thurston, guard
2005: Reggie White, defensive end
2009: Bob Harlan, president and CEO

34. The Packers purchased rain insurance for the October 8 game against Racine, which would pay the visiting team's guarantee if there was at least .1 inches. When it rained only .09 inches and the game drew few fans, it put the team in debt.

35. Gary Knafelc, who later became the stadium's public address announcer.

36. G Joe Andruzzi, Scottish Claymores; S Atari Bigby, Amsterdam Admirals; TE Tory Humphrey, Amsterdam Admirals; DE Cullen Jenkins, Cologne Centurions; LB George Koonce, Ohio Glory; LB Paris Lenon, Amsterdam Admirals; WR Ruvell Martin, Amsterdam Admirals; QB Craig Nall, Scottish Claymores; QB Doug Pederson, NY/NJ Knights, Rhein Fire; G Marco Rivera, Scottish Claymores; P B.J. Sander Hamburg, Sea Devils; WR Bill Schroeder, Rhein Fire; G/T Barry Stokes, Rhein Fire, Scottish Claymores; LB Nate Wayne, Barcelona Dragons; QB Danny Wuerffel, Rhein Fire

37. True

38. Buddy Aydelette, Birmingham Stallions; Robert Barber, Washington Federals; Bruce Beekley, Oakland Invaders; Ross Browner, Houston Gamblers; Mike Butler, Tampa Bay Bandits; Mossy Cade, Memphis Showboats; Paul Ott Carruth, Birmingham Stallions; Putt Choate, San Antonio Gunslingers; Chuck Clanton, Birmingham Stallions; Allan Clark, Arizona Wranglers; John Corker, Michigan Panthers; Rich Dimler, Los Angeles Express; Greg Feasel, Denver Gold; Nolan Franz, Boston Breakers; Chuck Fusina, Philadelphia Stars; David Greenwood, Michigan Panthers; Bob Gruber, Jacksonville Bulls; Joey Hackett, San Antonio Gunslingers; Jim Hargrove, Boston Breakers, Michigan Panthers; Perry Hartnett, Chicago Blitz; Jerry Holmes, Pittsburgh Maulers; Van Jakes, Jacksonville Bulls; Ken Johnson, New Jersey Generals; Perry Kemp, Jacksonville Bulls; Kit Lathrop, Arizona Wranglers; Sean Landeta, Philadelphia Stars; Bobby Leopold, New Jersey Generals; Gary Lewis, Chicago Blitz; Von Mansfield, Michigan Panthers; Charles Martin, Birmingham Stallions; Larry Mason, Jacksonville Bulls; Aubrey Matthews, Jacksonville Bulls; Terdell Middleton, Memphis Showboats; Keith Millard, Jacksonville Bulls; John Miller, New Jersey Generals; Jim Bob Morris, San Antonio Gunslingers; Bob Nelson, Omaha Outlaws; Brad Oates, Philadelphia Stars; Steve Pisarkiewicz, Orlando Renegades; Larry Rubens, Memphis Showboats; Dave Pureifory, Birmingham Stallions; Alan Risher, Arizona Wranglers; Tommy Robison, Houston Gamblers; Dan Ross, New Orleans Breakers; Dave Simmons, Arizona Outlaws; Carl Sullivan, Oakland Invaders; John Sullivan, Oakland Invaders; Mickey Sutton, Birmingham Stallions, Pittsburgh Maulers; Harry Sydney, Memphis Showboats; Arland Thompson, San Antonio Gunslingers; John Thompson, Oakland Invaders; Walter Tullis, New Jersey Generals; Mike Weddington, New Jersey Generals; Reggie White, Memphis Showboats

39. Offense: Bart Starr, quarterback; Jim Taylor, fullback; Paul Hornung, halfback; Don Hutson, receiver; James Lofton, receiver; Sterling Sharpe, receiver; Forrest Gregg, tackle; Cal Hubbard, tackle; Gale Gillingham, guard; Jerry Kramer, guard; Jim Ringo, center

40. Defense: Cal Hubbard, lineman; Reggie White, defensive end; Willie Davis, defensive end; Henry Jordan, defensive tackle; Ray Nitschke, linebacker; Dave Robinson, linebacker; Fred Carr, linebacker; Herb Adderley, cornerback; Willie Buchanon, cornerback; Bobby Dillon, safety; Willie Wood, safety

41. Special teams: Travis Williams, kick returner; Billy Grimes, punt returner; Chris Jacke, kicker; Craig Hentrich, punter

42. Vince Lombardi and Don Hutson

(Getty Images)

About the Author

Christopher Walsh has been an award-winning sportswriter since 1990, and currently covers the University of Alabama football program for BamaOnline.com. He's twice been nominated for a Pulitzer Prize, won three Football Writers Association of America awards, and received the 2006 Herby Kirby Memorial Award, the Alabama Sports Writers Association's highest honor. Originally from Minnesota and a graduate of the University of New Hampshire, he currently resides in Tuscaloosa.

To make comments, suggestions or share an idea with the author, go to http://whosno1.blogspot.com/.

The author would like to thank Tom Bast for spearheading this project, and everyone at Triumph Books who worked on it.